MAY 50 COLORING PAGES
FOR OLDER KIDS RELAXATION

SHIH CHIEN HUA

PUBLISHED BY:
SHIH CHIEN HUA
Copyright © 2018

SEABIRD SHOP >50FOR

FB FAN PAGE

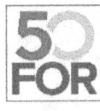

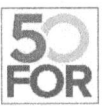

All rights reserved.
No part of this publication may be copied, reproduced in any format, by any means, electronic or otherwise, without prior consent from the copyright owner and publisher of this book.

Disclaimer
The information contained in this book is for general information purposes only. The information is provided by the authors and while we endeavor to keep the information up to date and correct, we make no representations or warranties of any kind, express or implied, about the completeness, accuracy, reliability, suitability or availability with respect to the book or the information, products, services, or related graphics contained in the book for any purpose. Any reliance you place on such information is therefore strictly at your own risk.

MAY 1ST

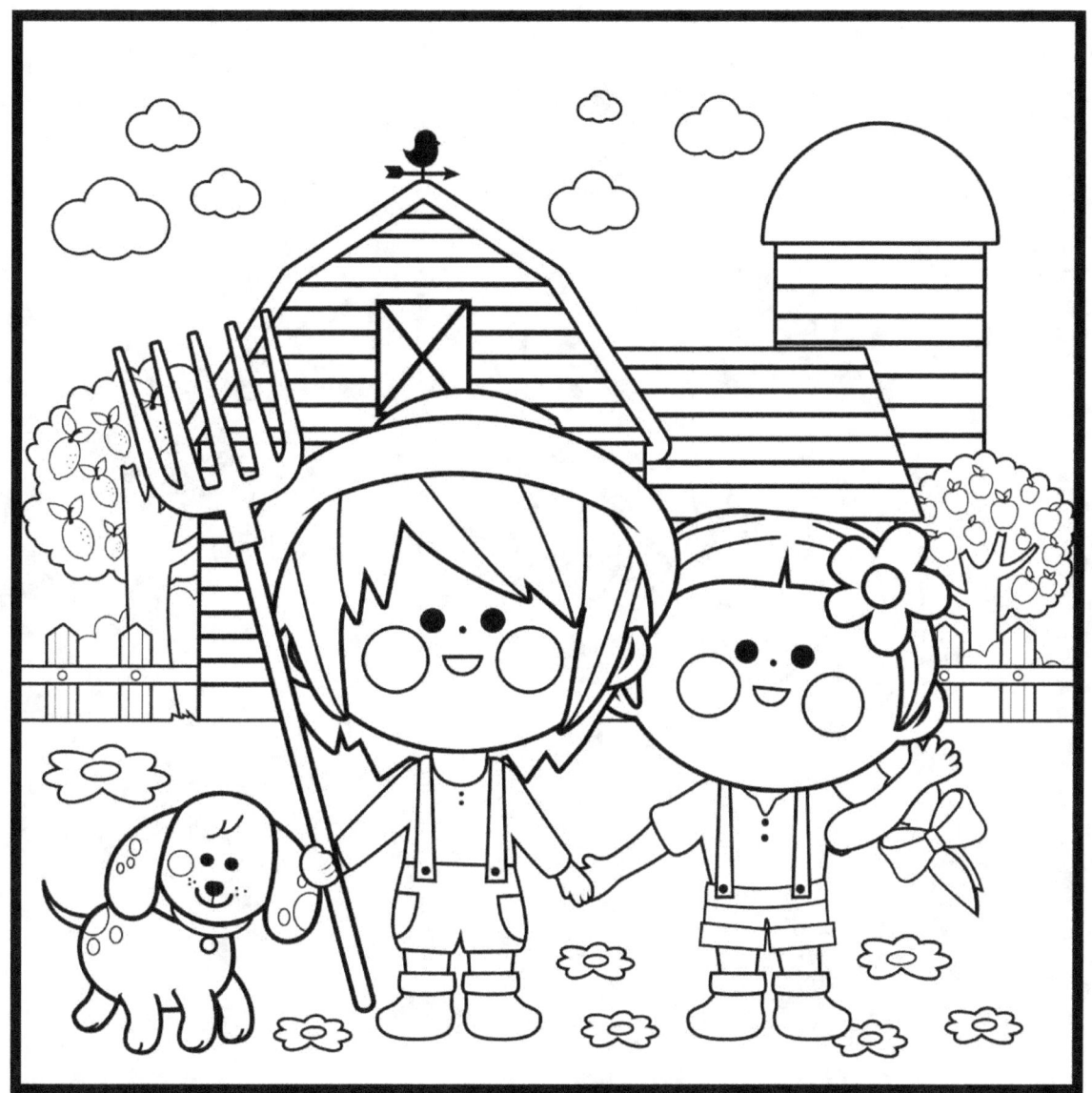

note:

_____

_____

_____

MAY 2ND

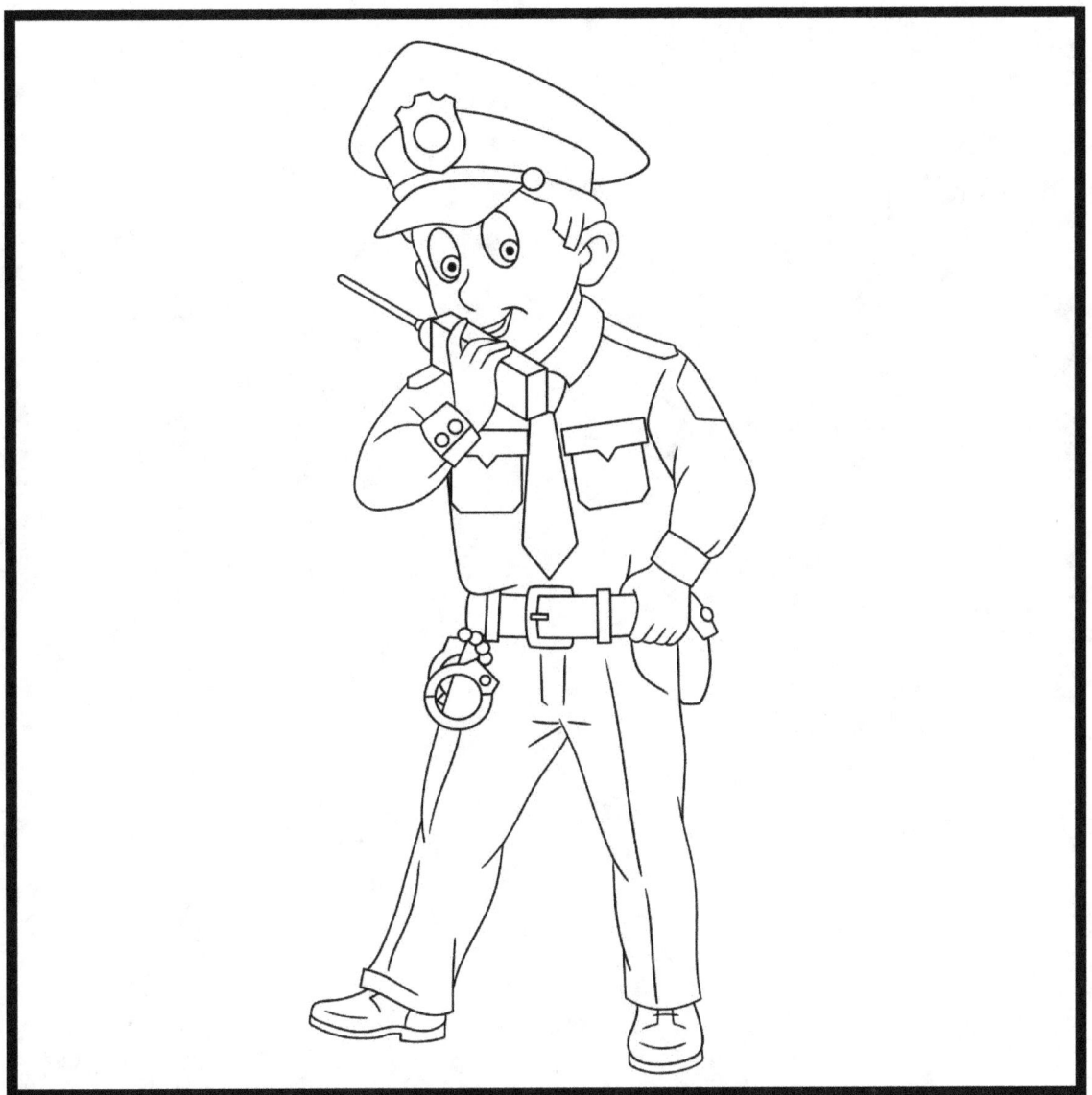

note:

_____

_____

_____

MAY 3RD

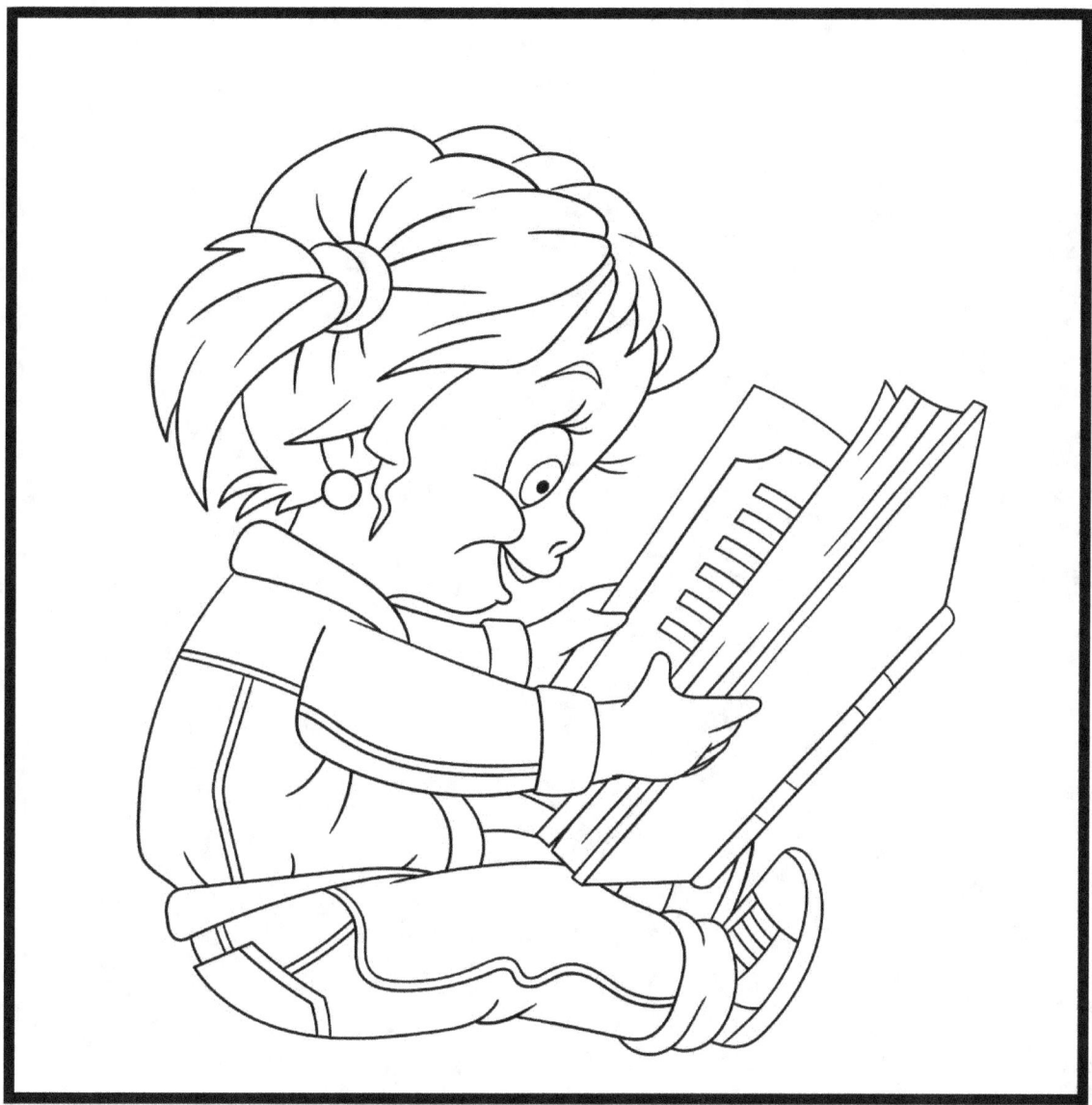

note:

_____

_____

_____

MAY 4TH

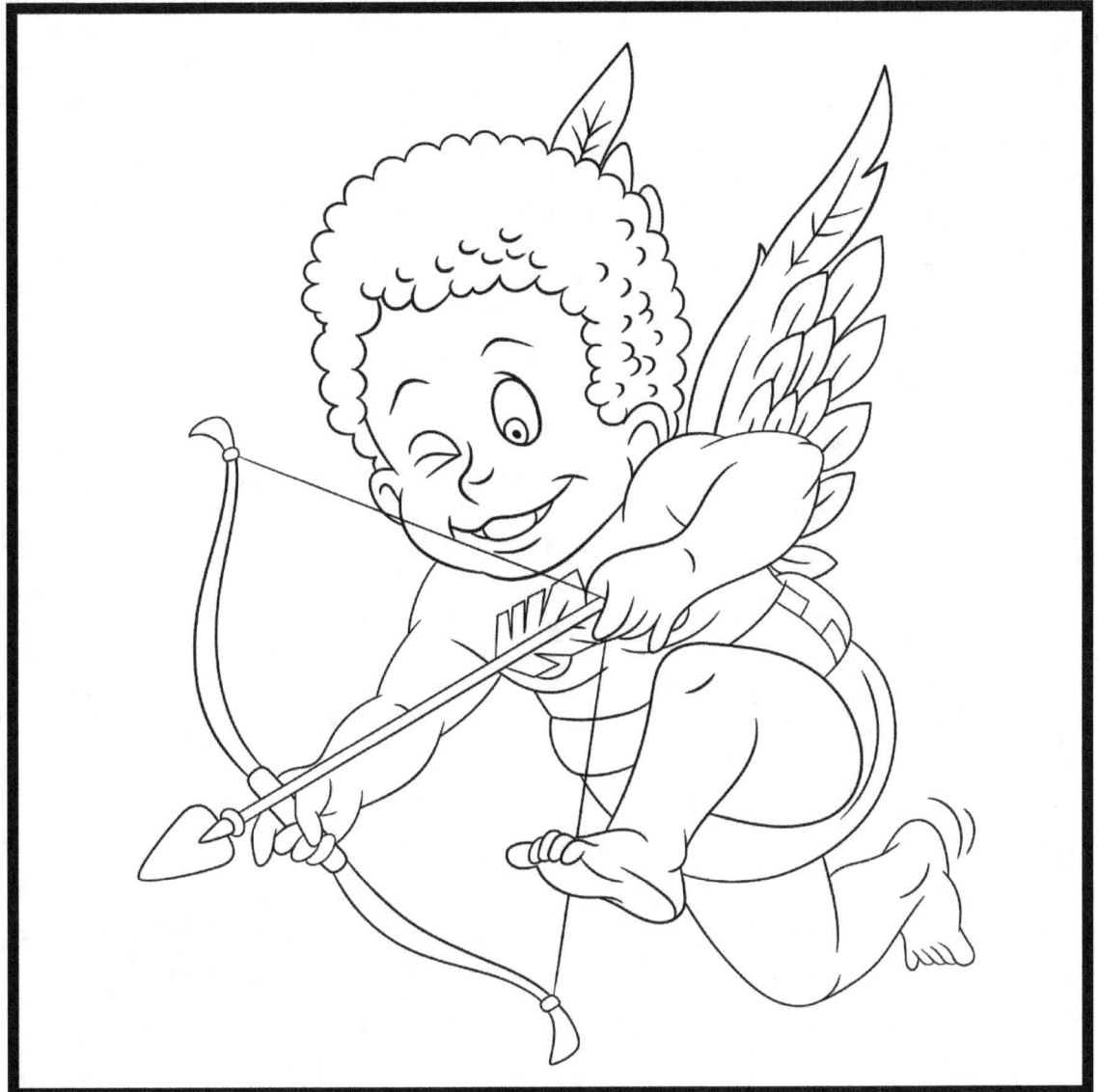

note:

_____

_____

_____

MAY 5TH

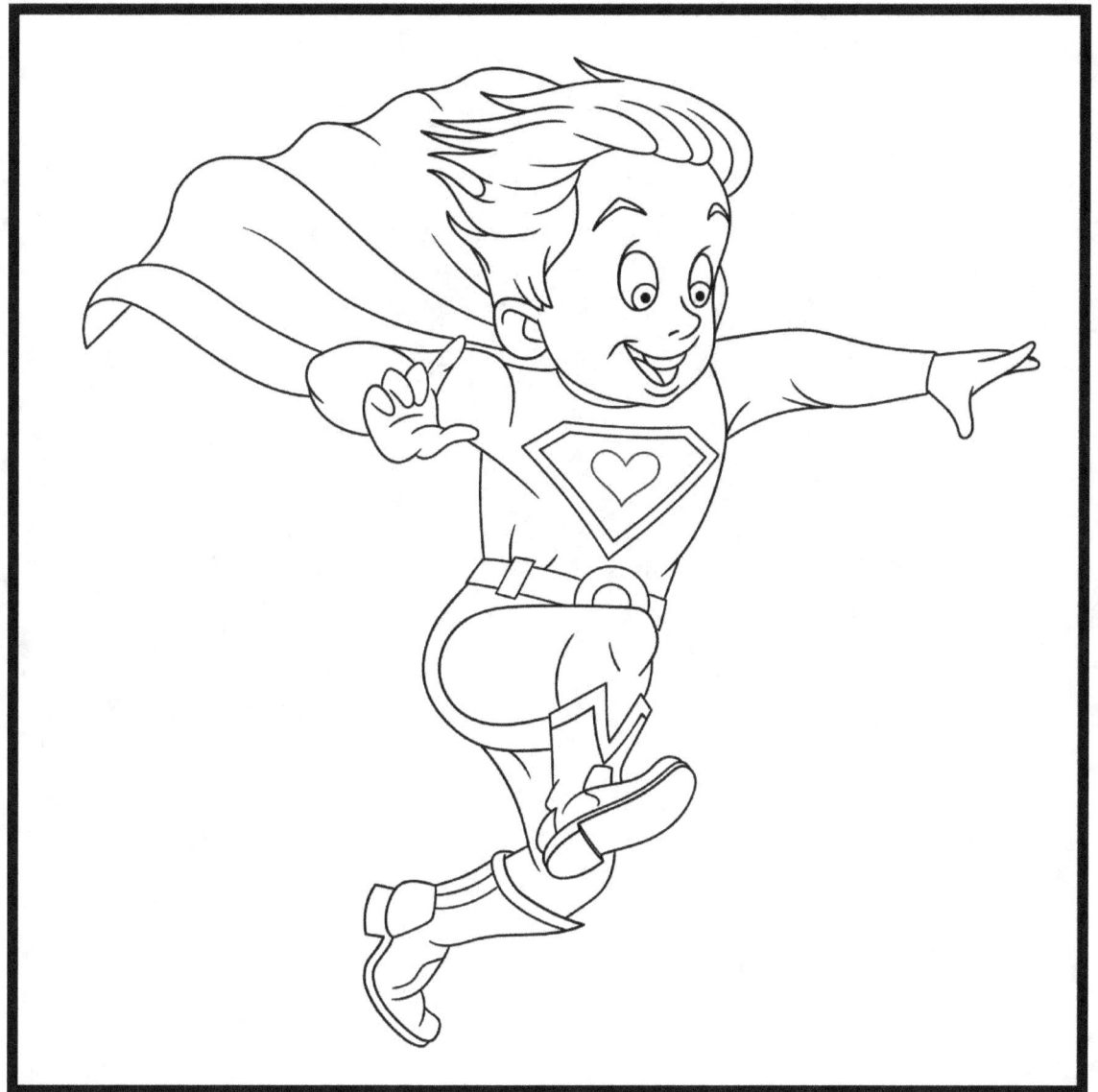

note:

_____

_____

_____

MAY 6TH

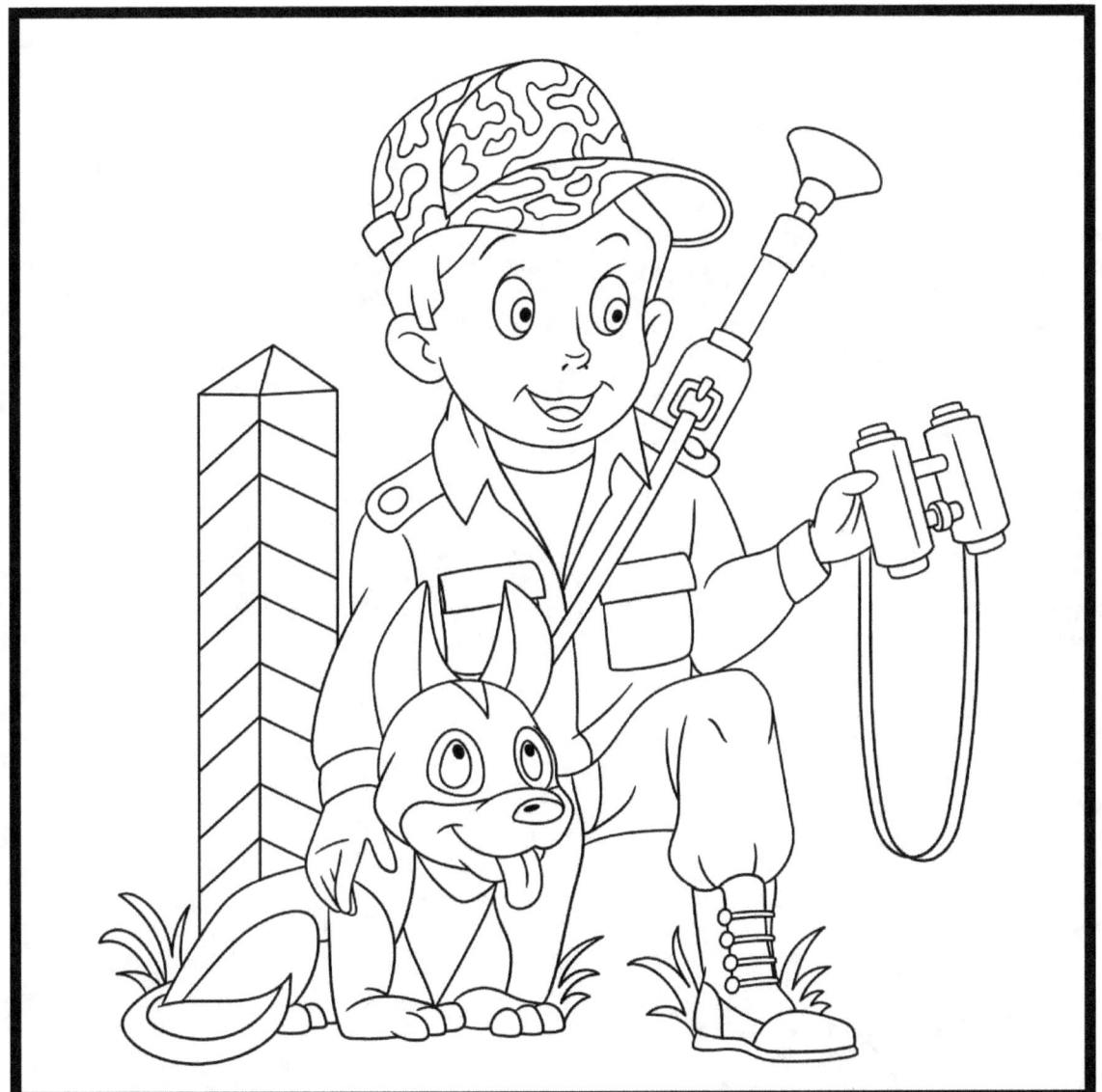

note:

_____

_____

_____

MAY 7TH

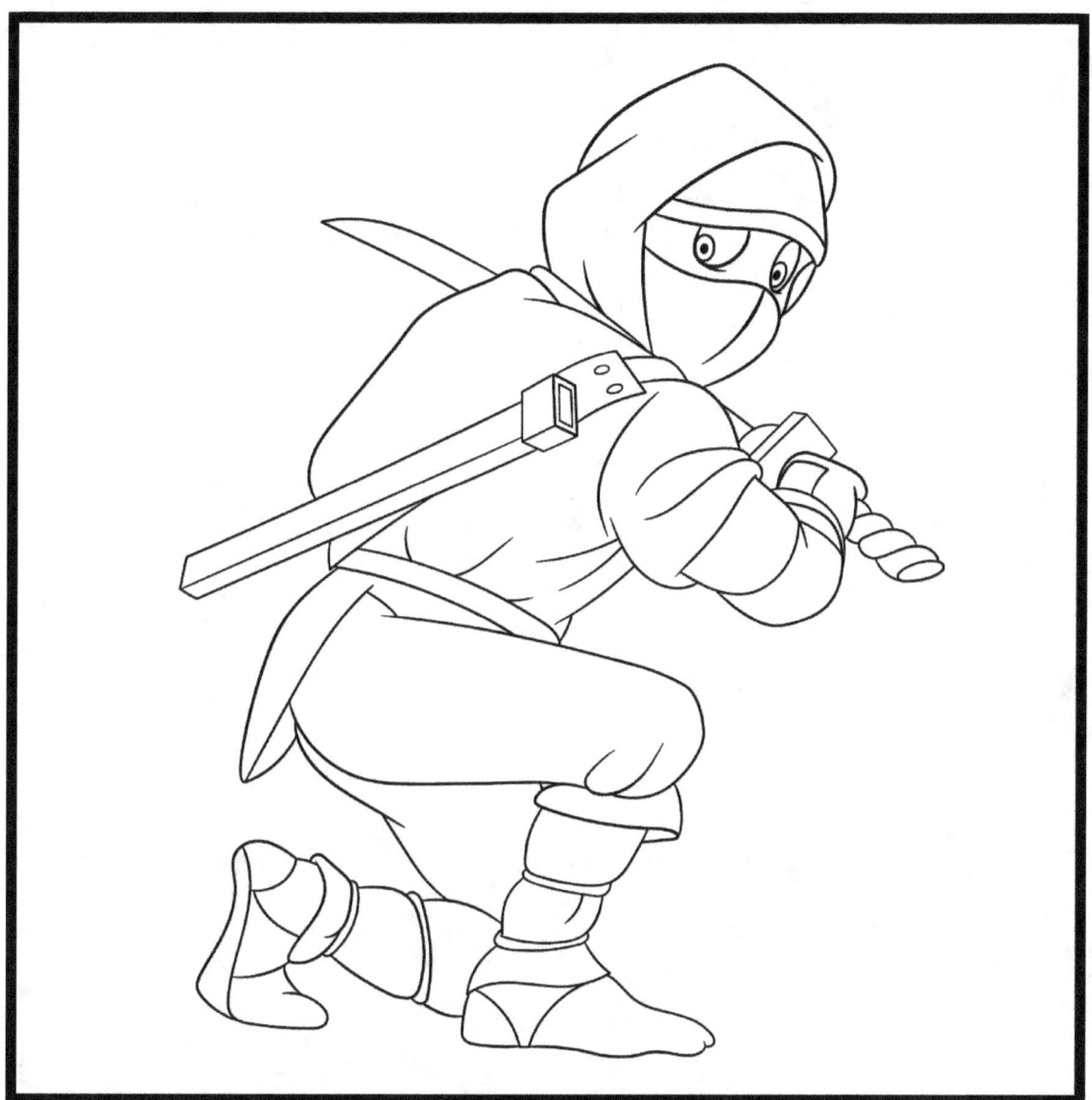

note:

_____

_____

_____

MAY 8TH

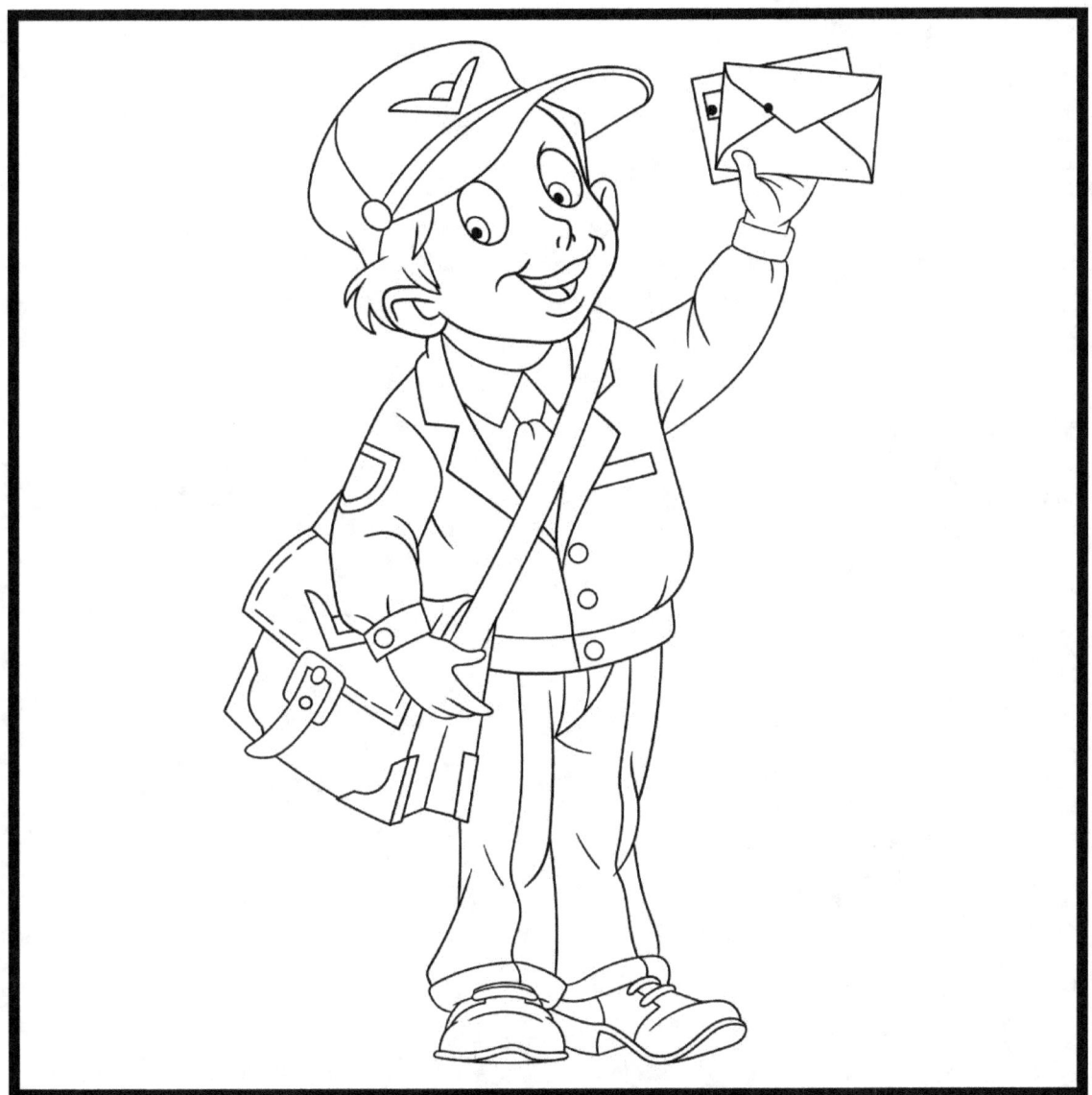

note:

_____

_____

_____

MAY 9TH

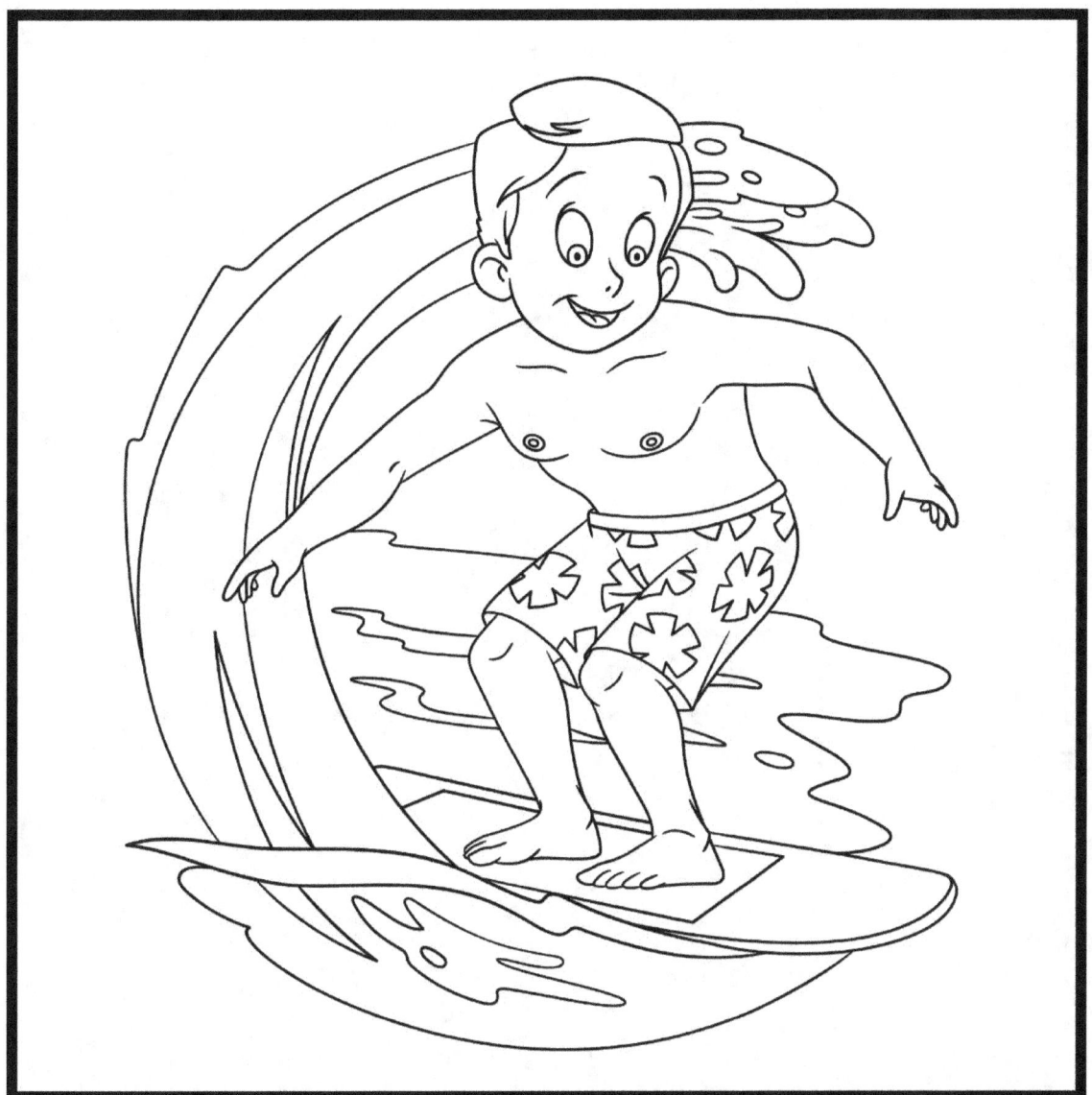

note:

_____

_____

_____

MAY 10TH

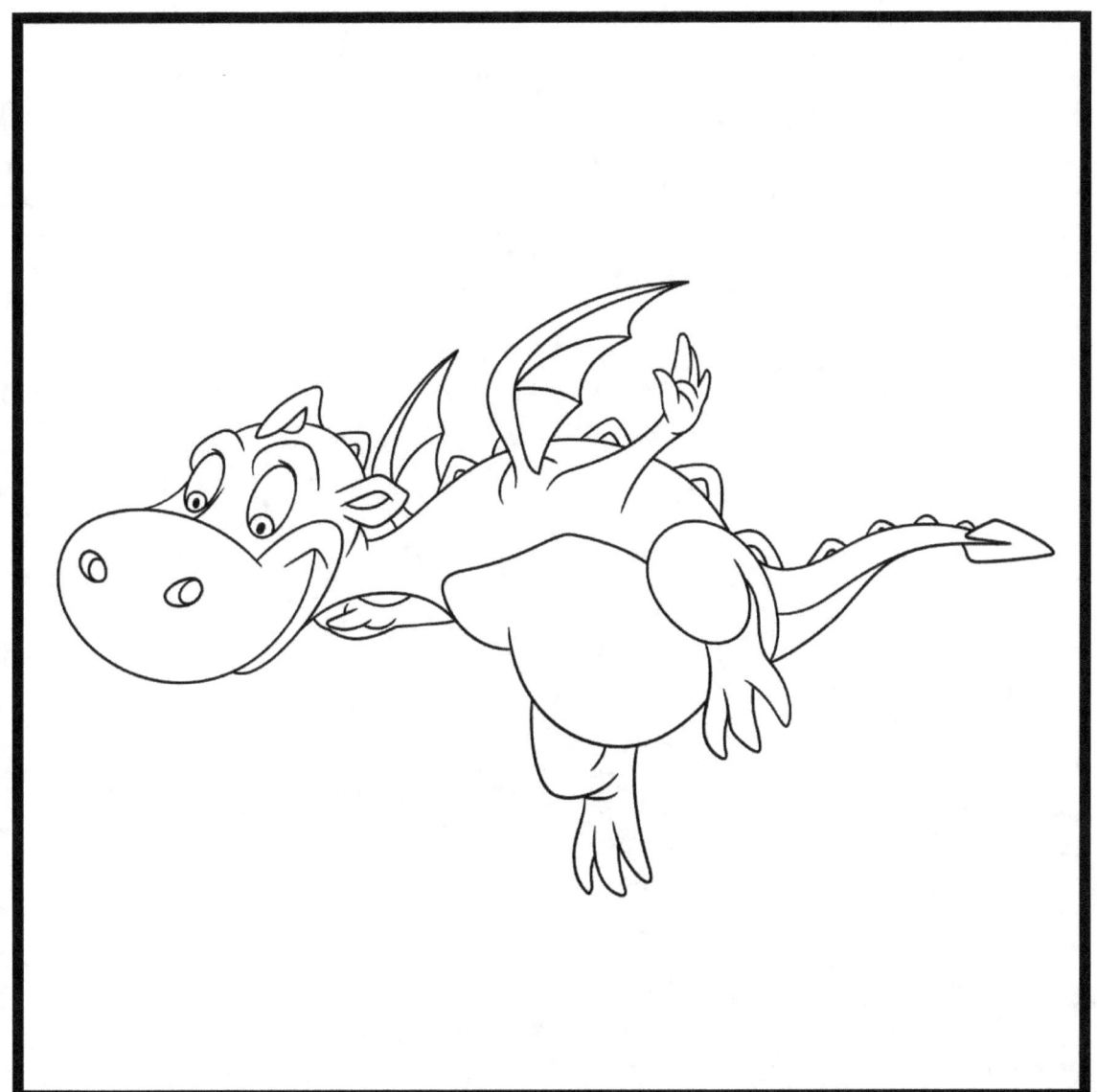

note:

_____

_____

_____

MAY 11TH

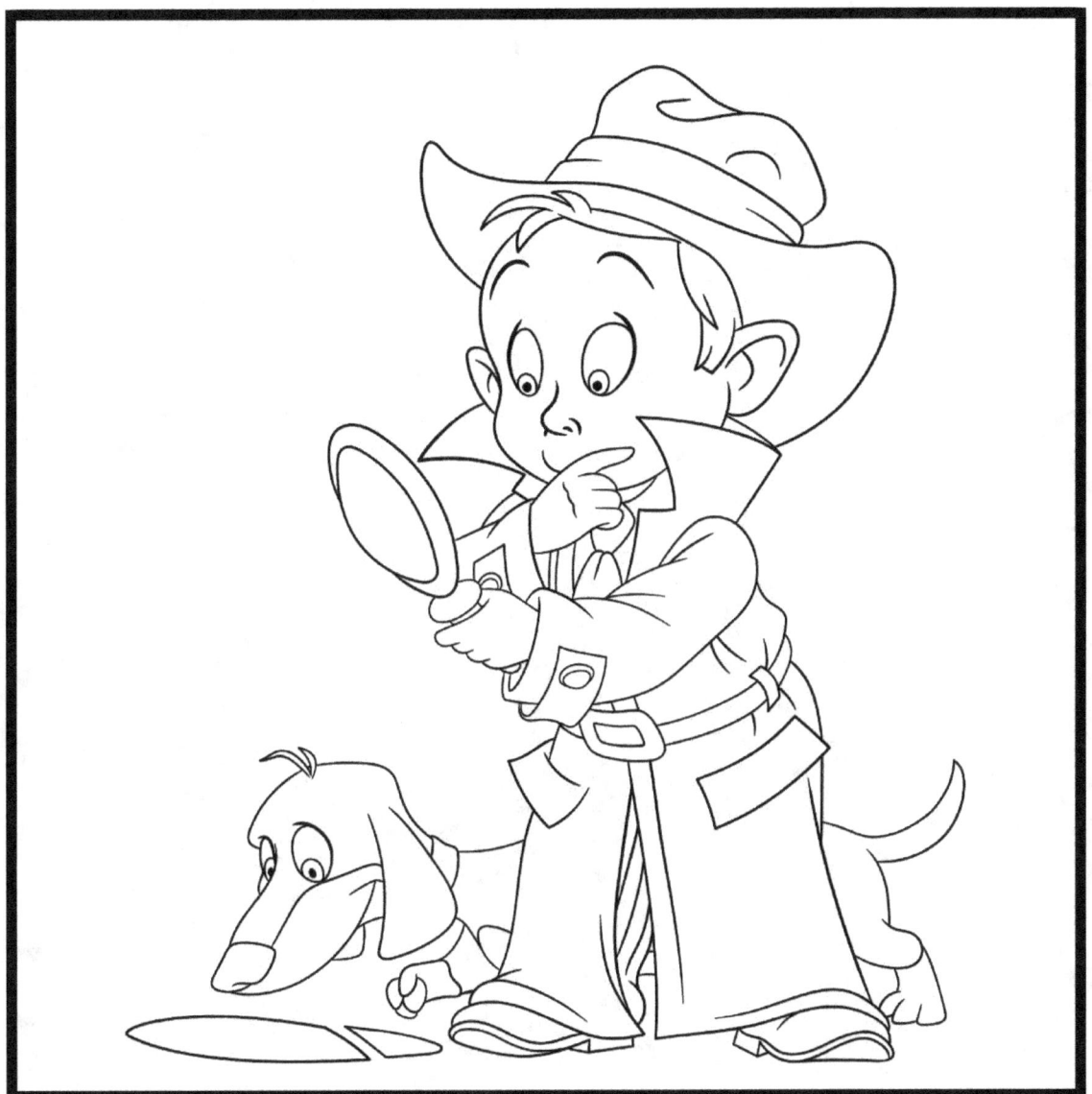

note:

_____

_____

_____

MAY 12TH

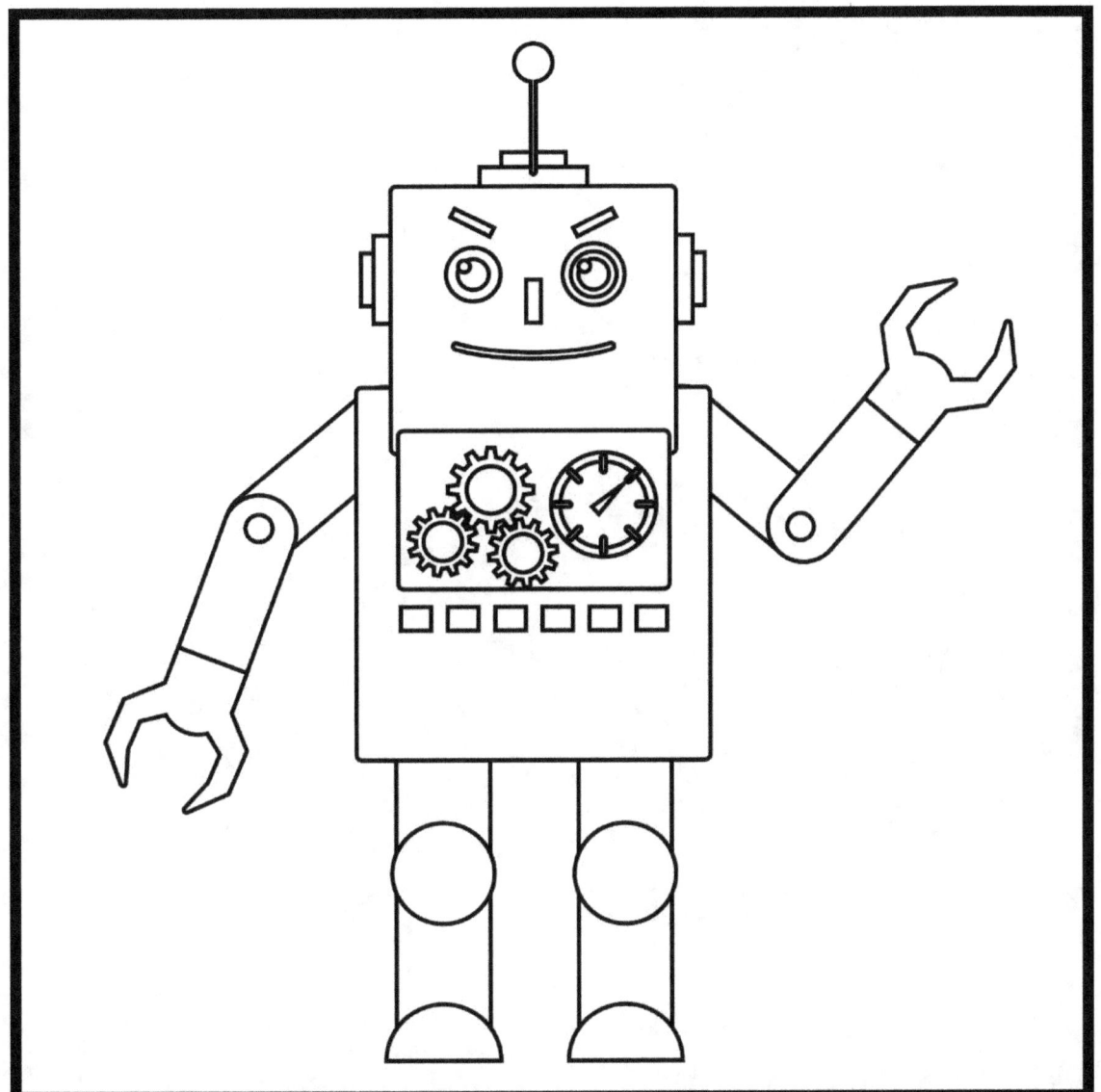

note:

_____

_____

_____

MAY 13TH

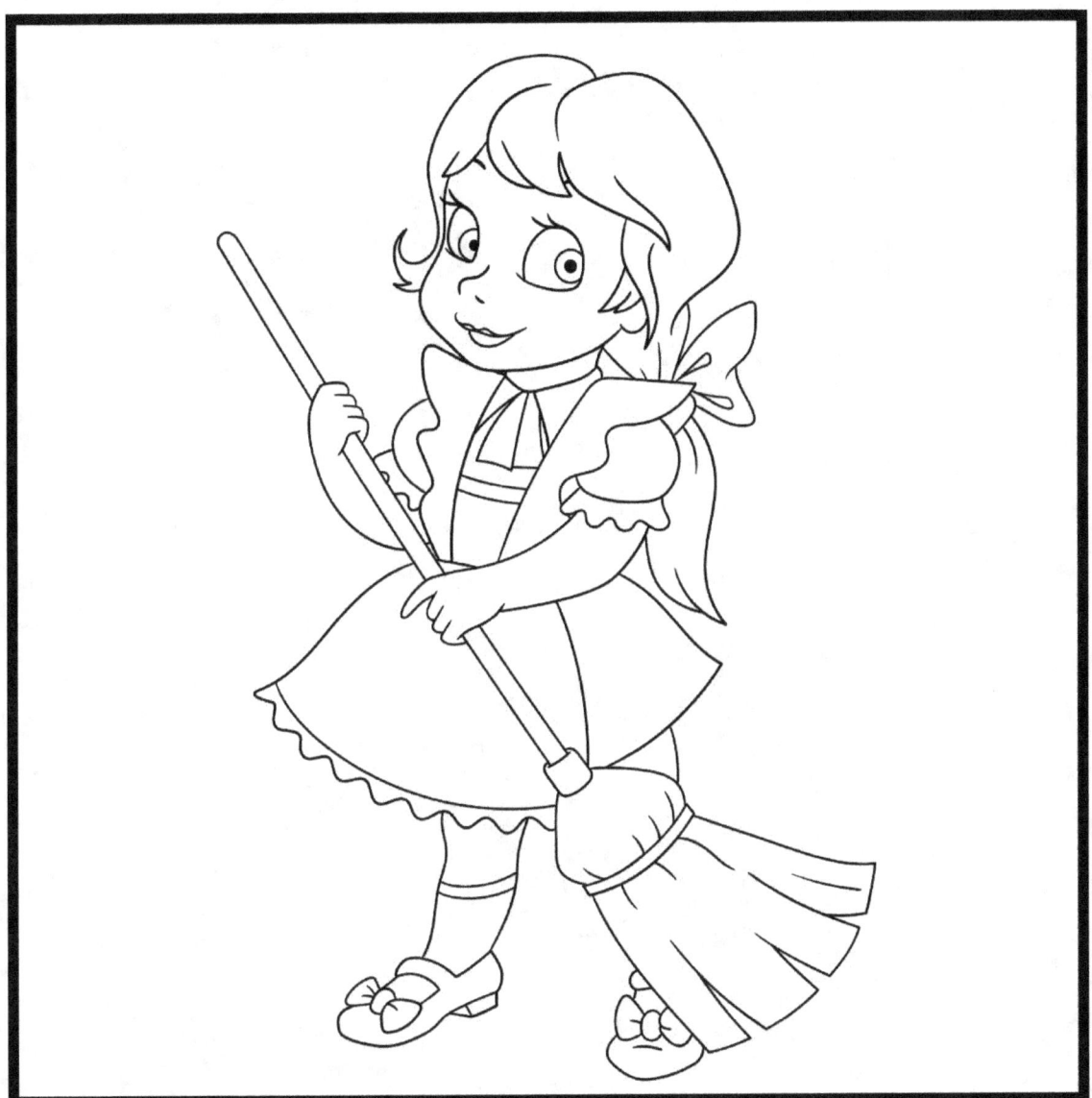

note:

_____

_____

_____

MAY 14TH

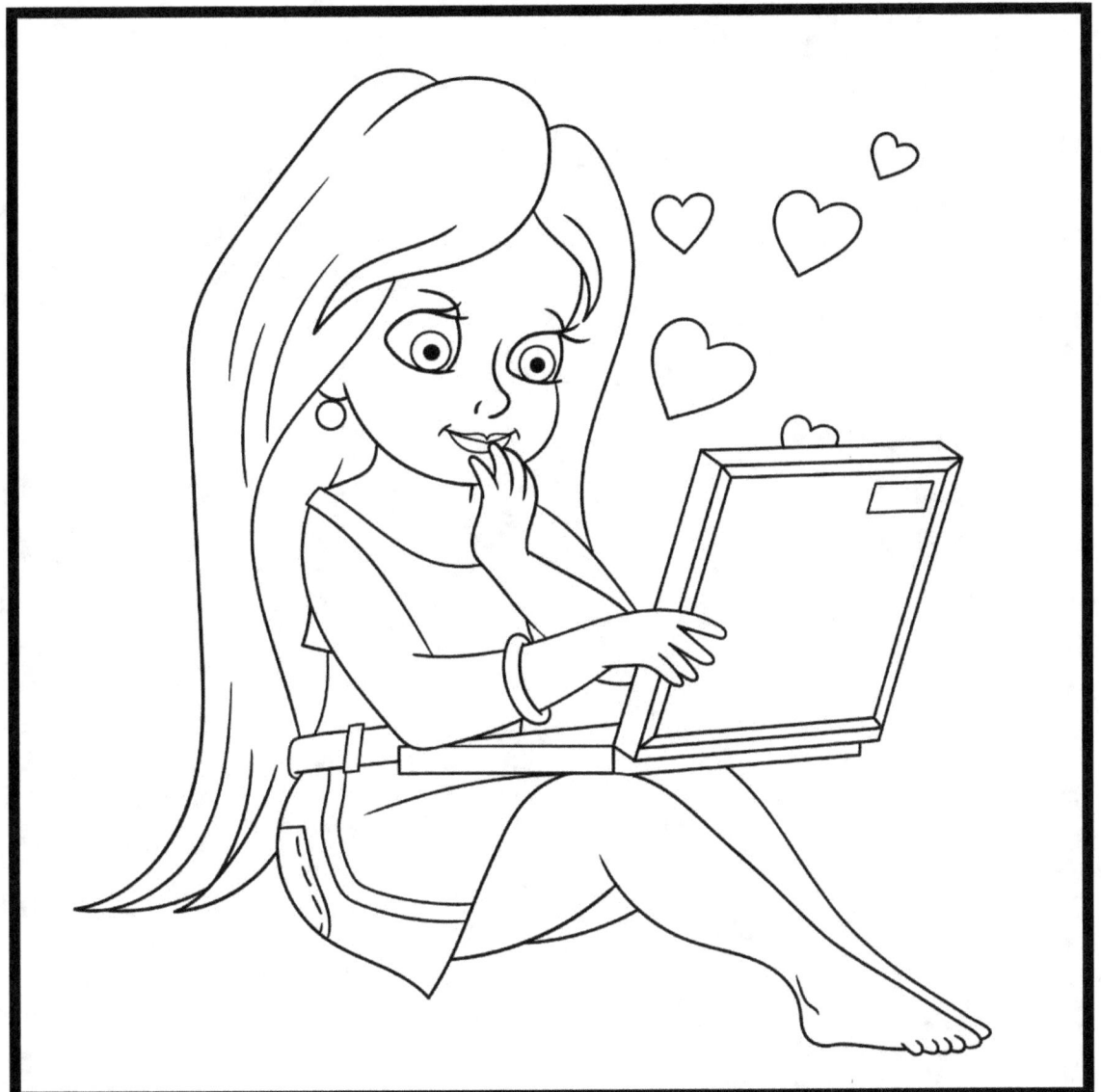

note:

_____

_____

_____

MAY 15TH

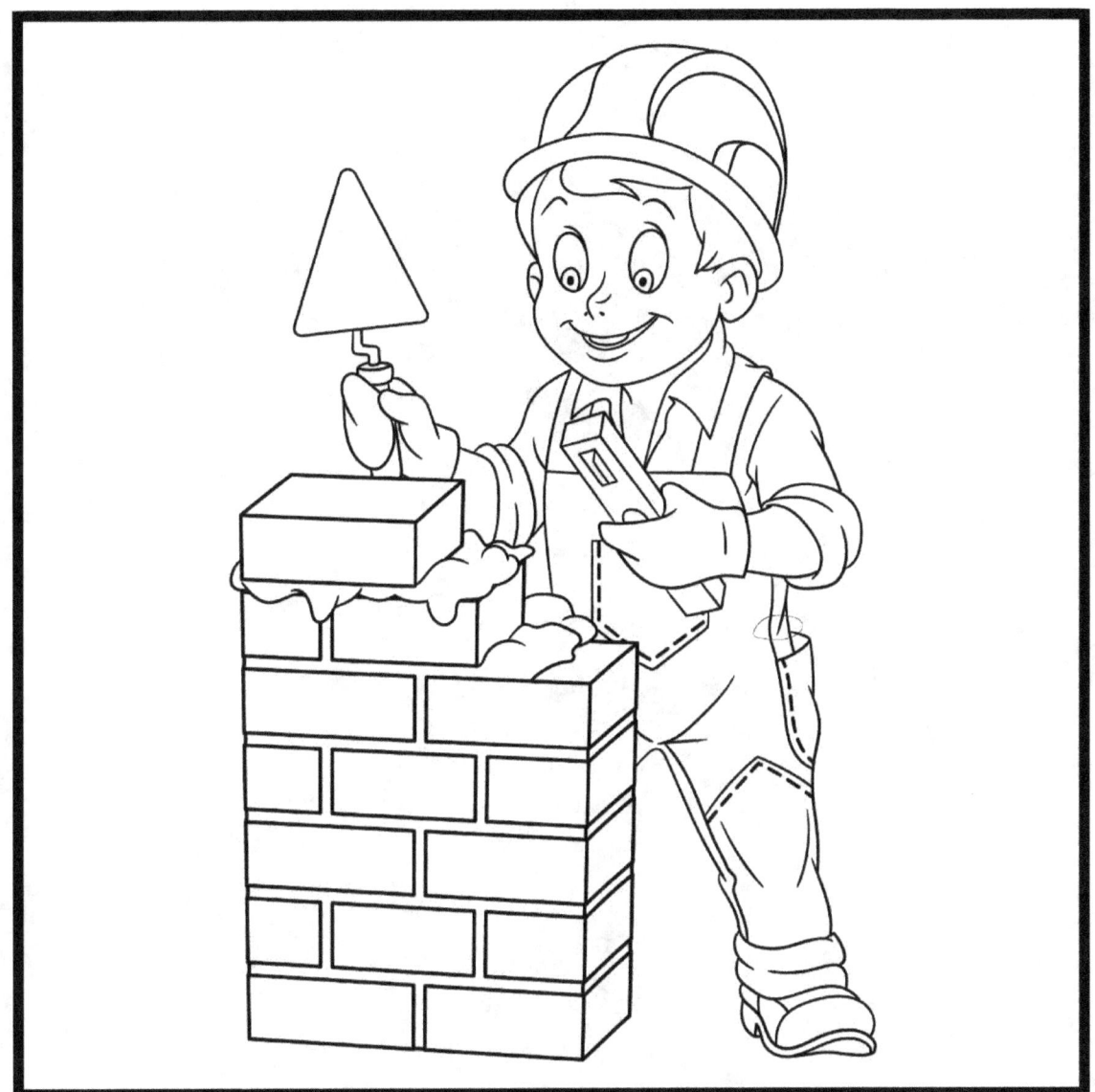

note:

_____

_____

_____

MAY 16TH

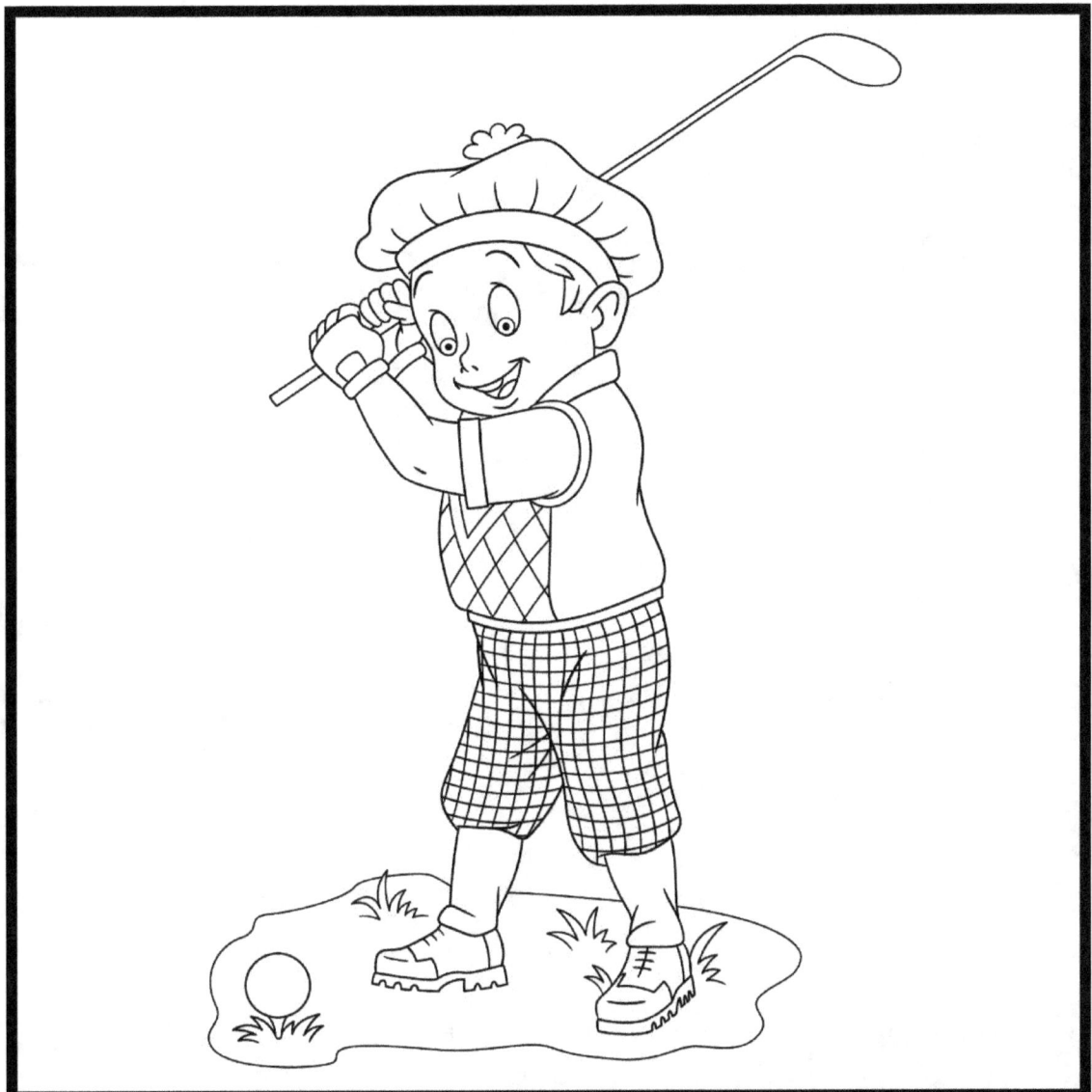

note:

_____

_____

_____

MAY 17TH

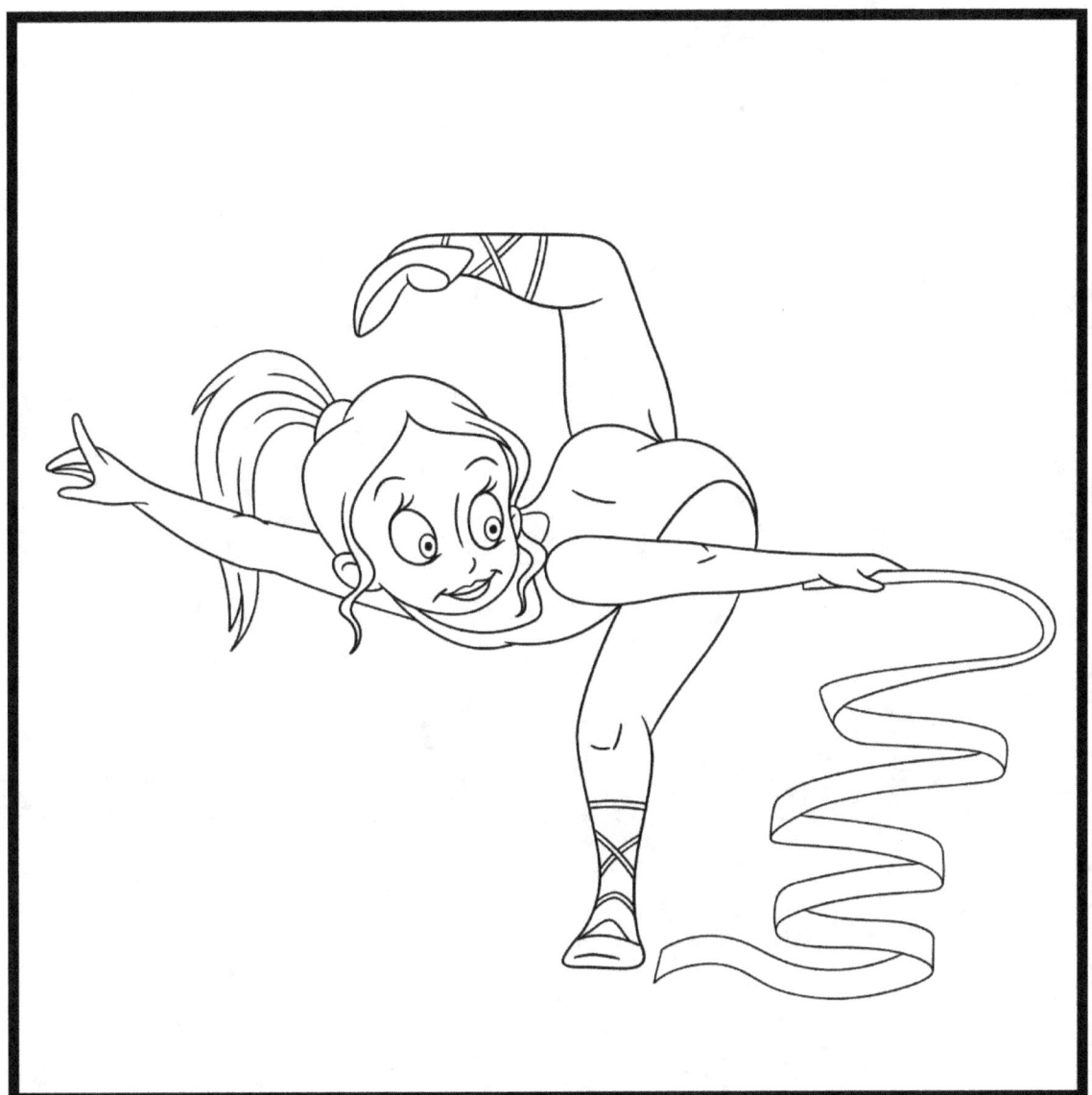

note:

_____

_____

_____

MAY 18TH

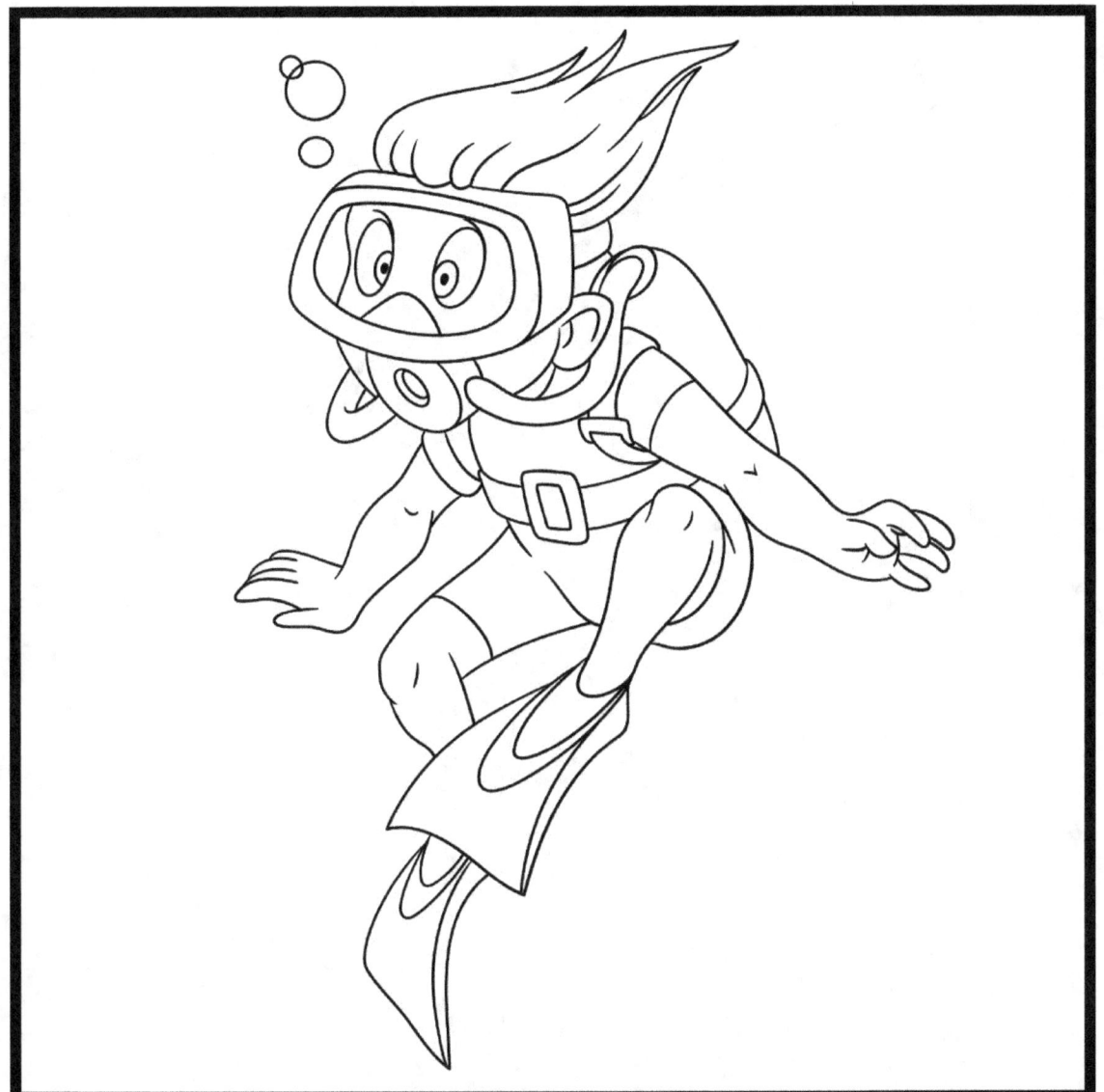

note:

_____

_____

_____

MAY 19TH

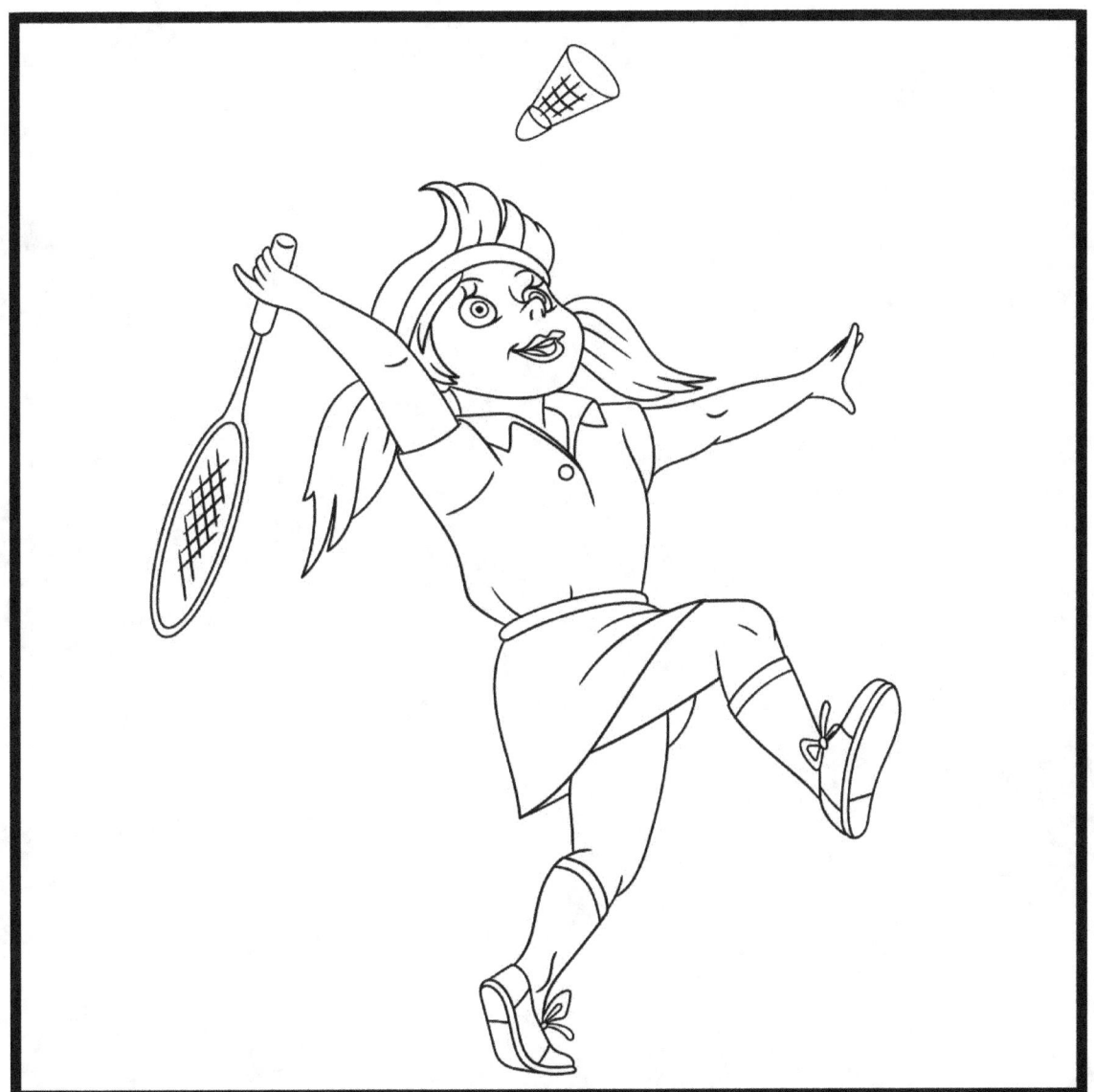

note:

_____

_____

_____

MAY 20TH

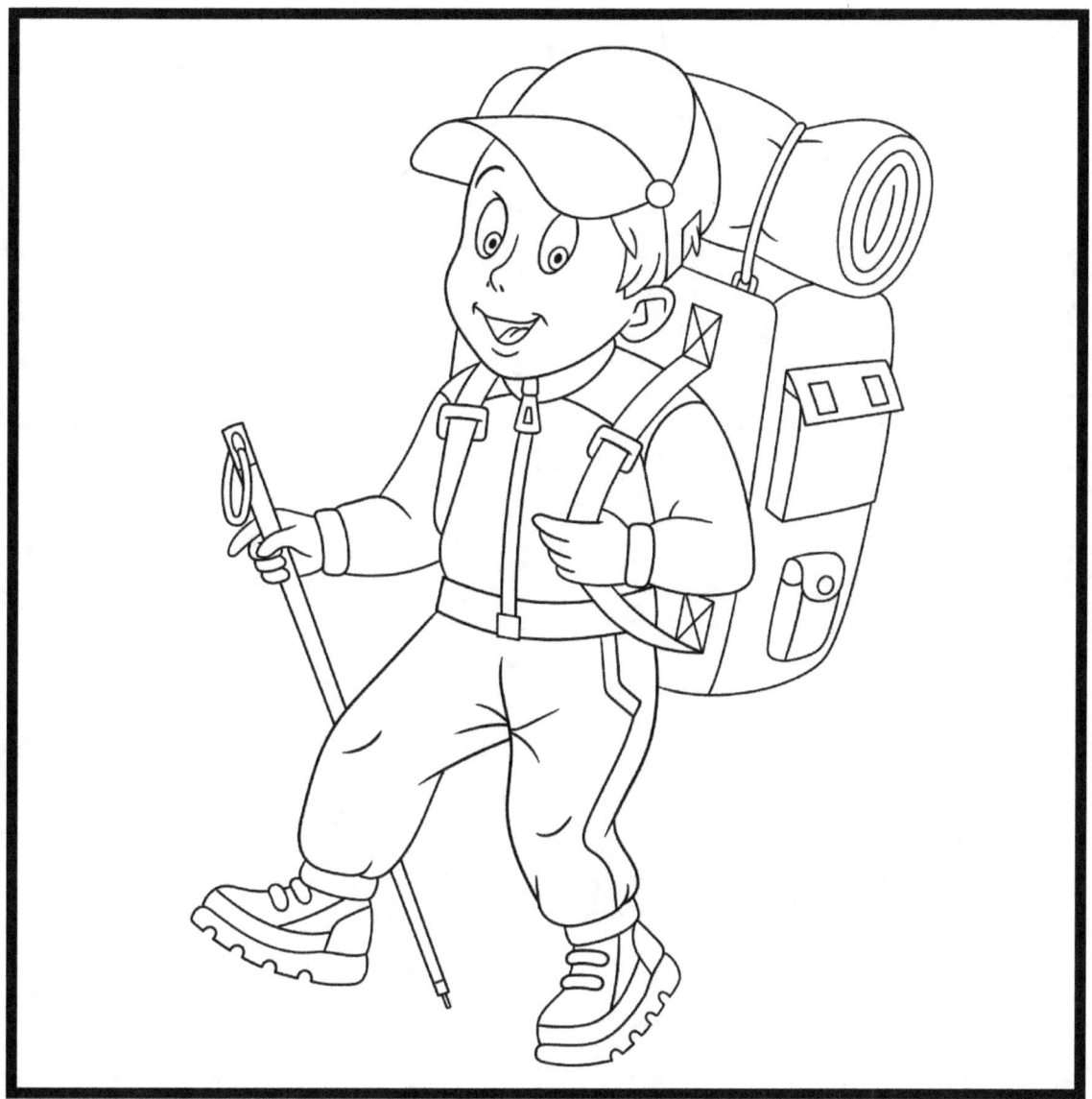

note:

_____

_____

_____

MAY 21TH

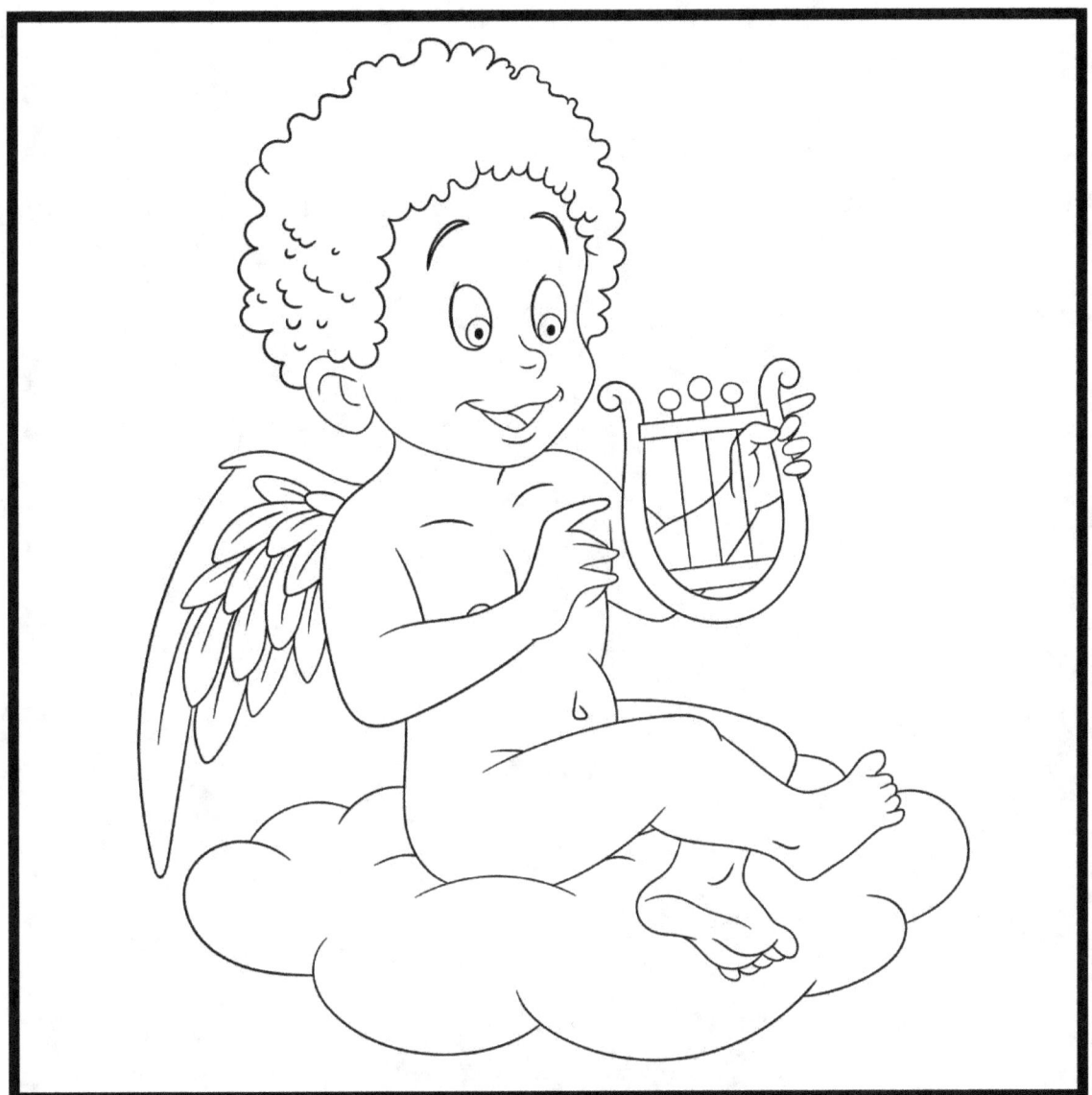

note:

_____

_____

_____

MAY 22TH

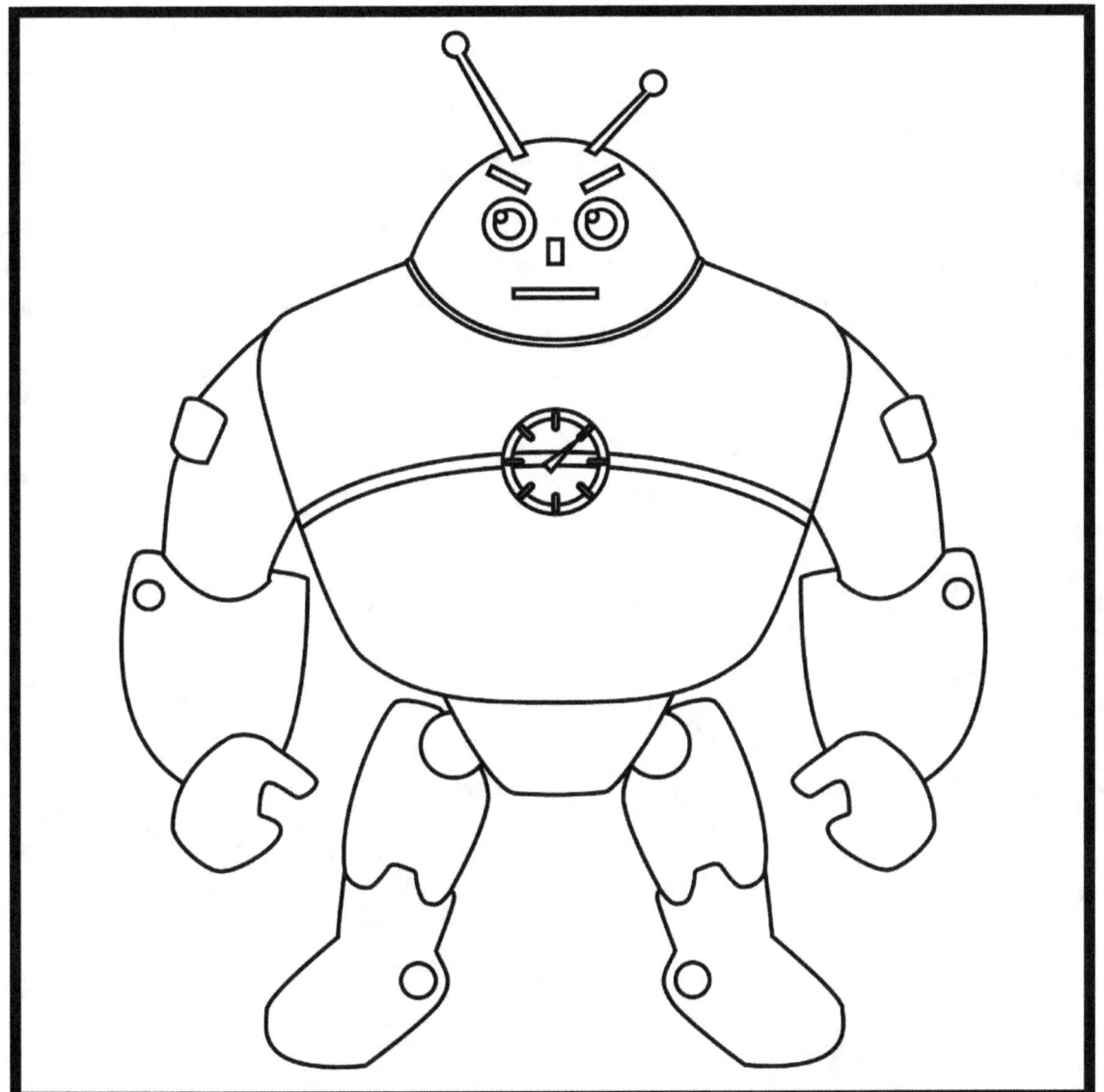

note:

_____

_____

_____

MAY 23TH

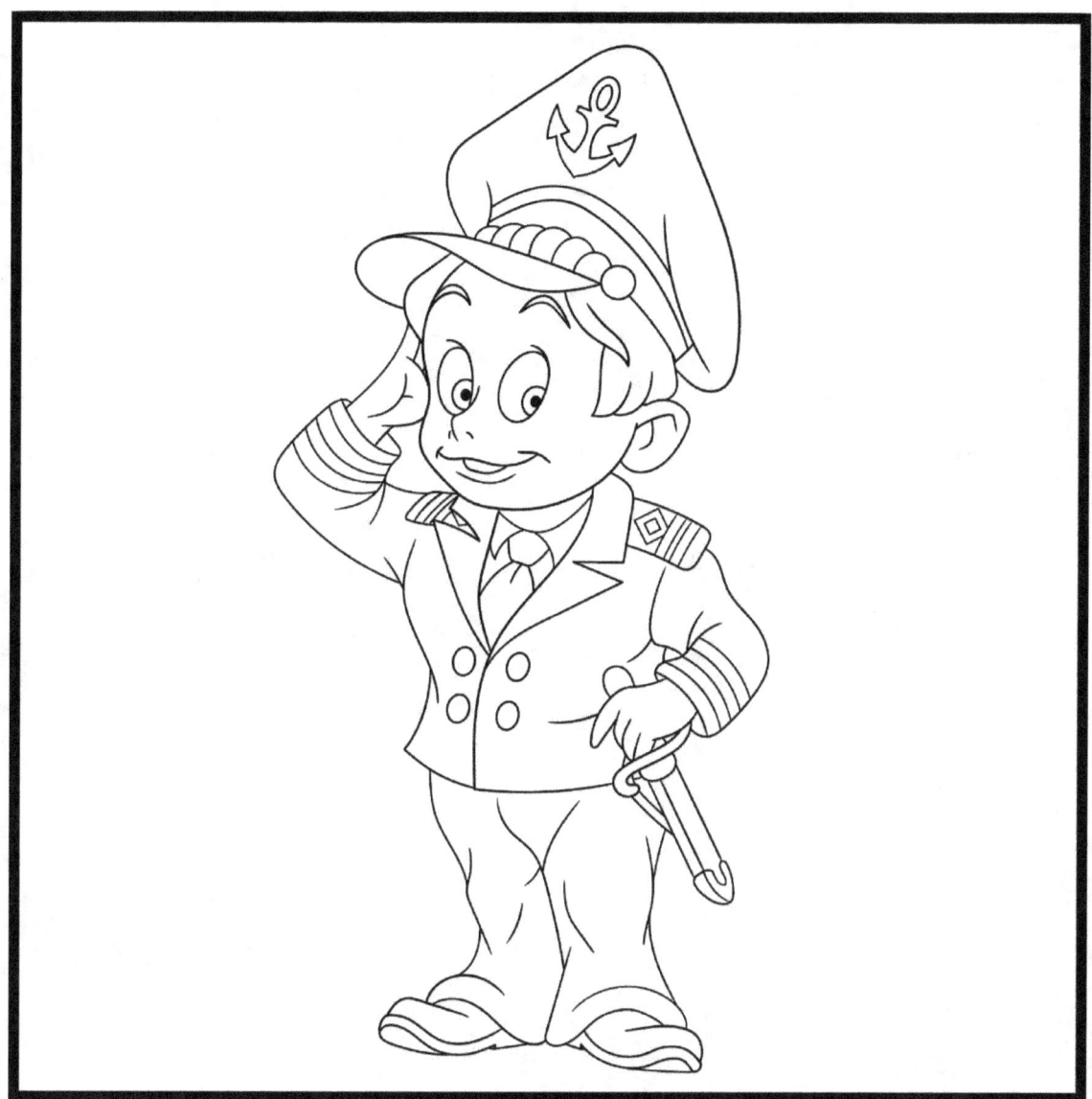

note:

_____

_____

_____

MAY 24TH

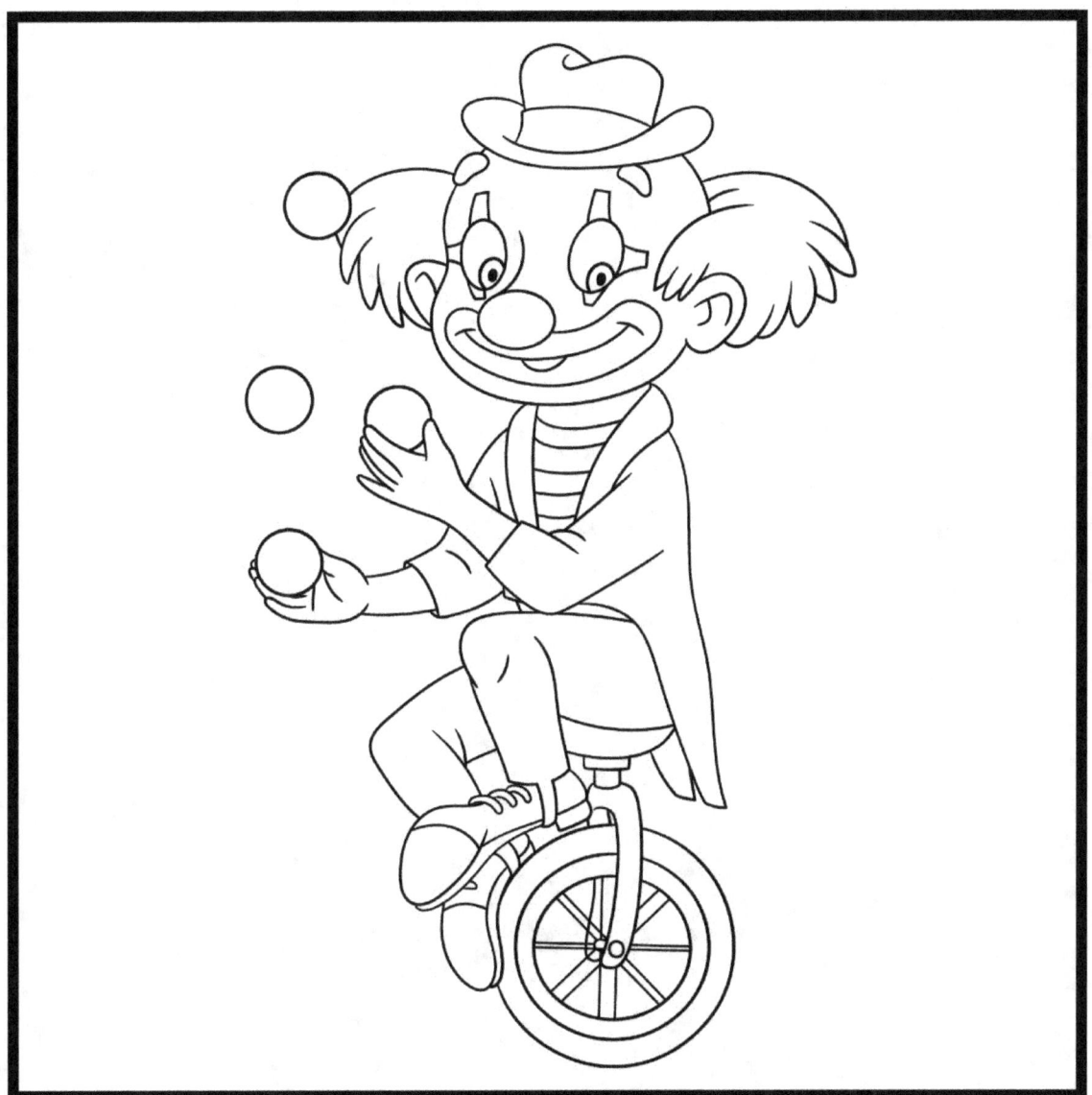

note:

_____

_____

_____

MAY 25TH

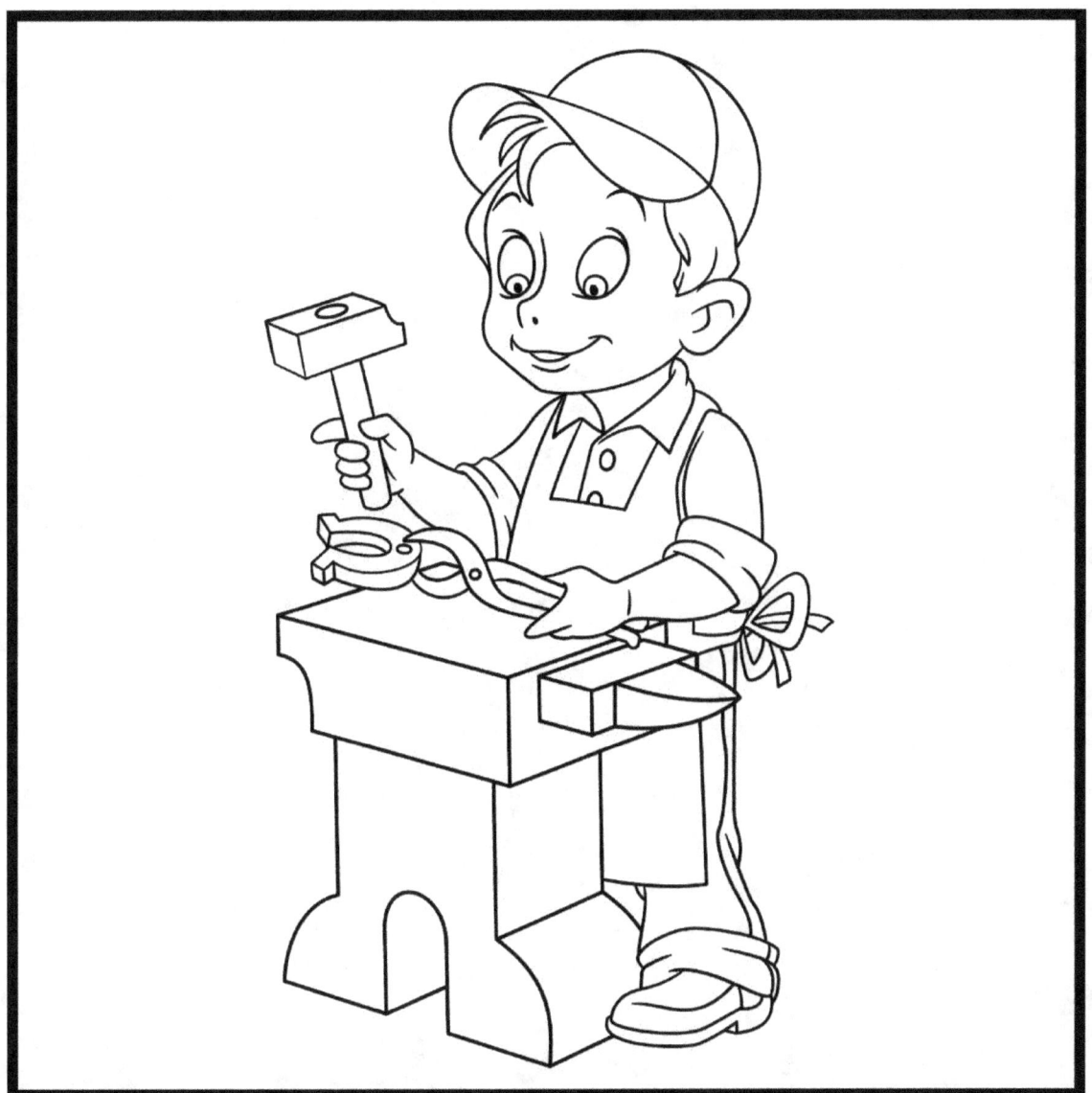

note:

_____

_____

_____

MAY 26TH

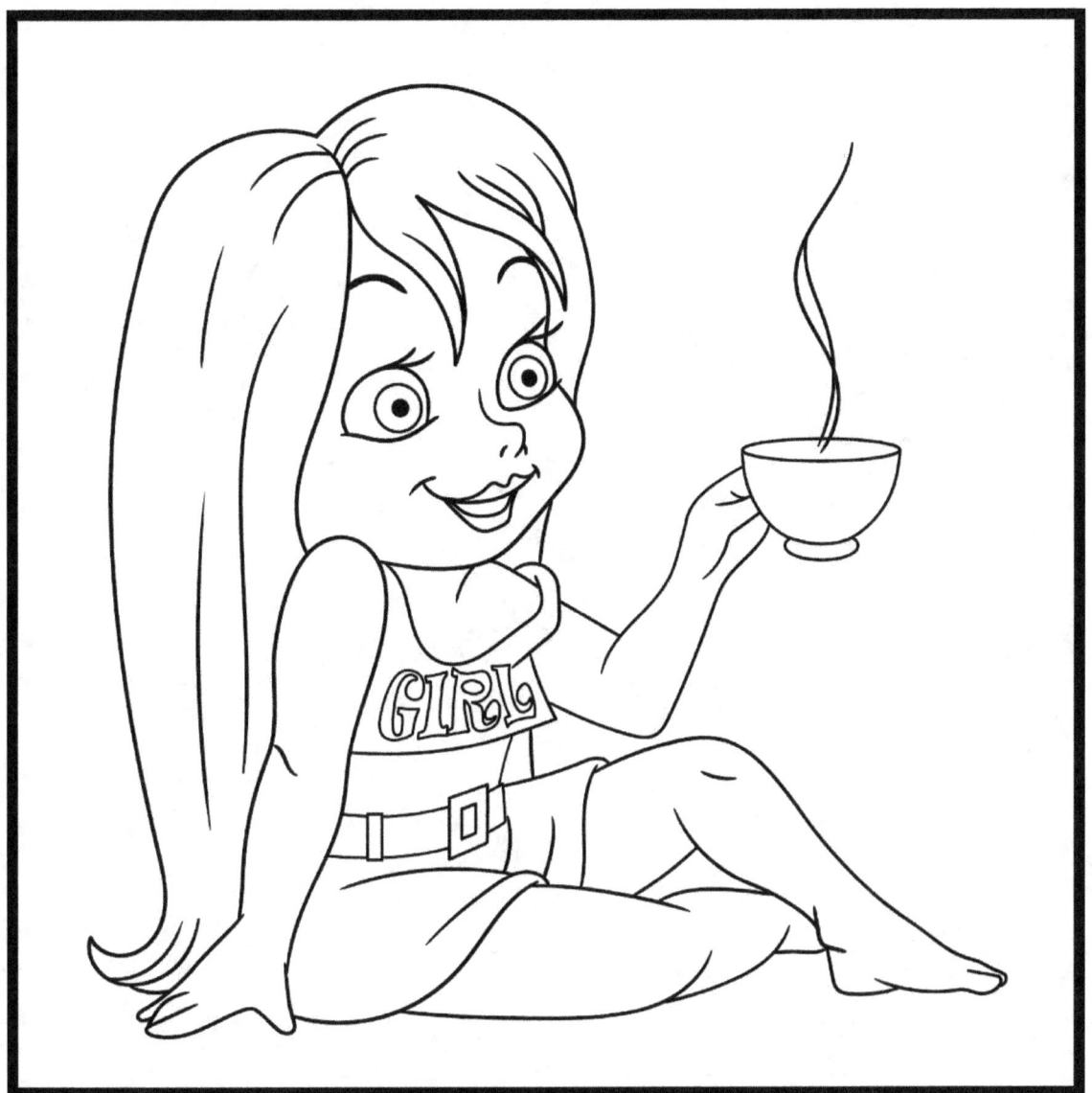

note:

_____

_____

_____

MAY 27TH

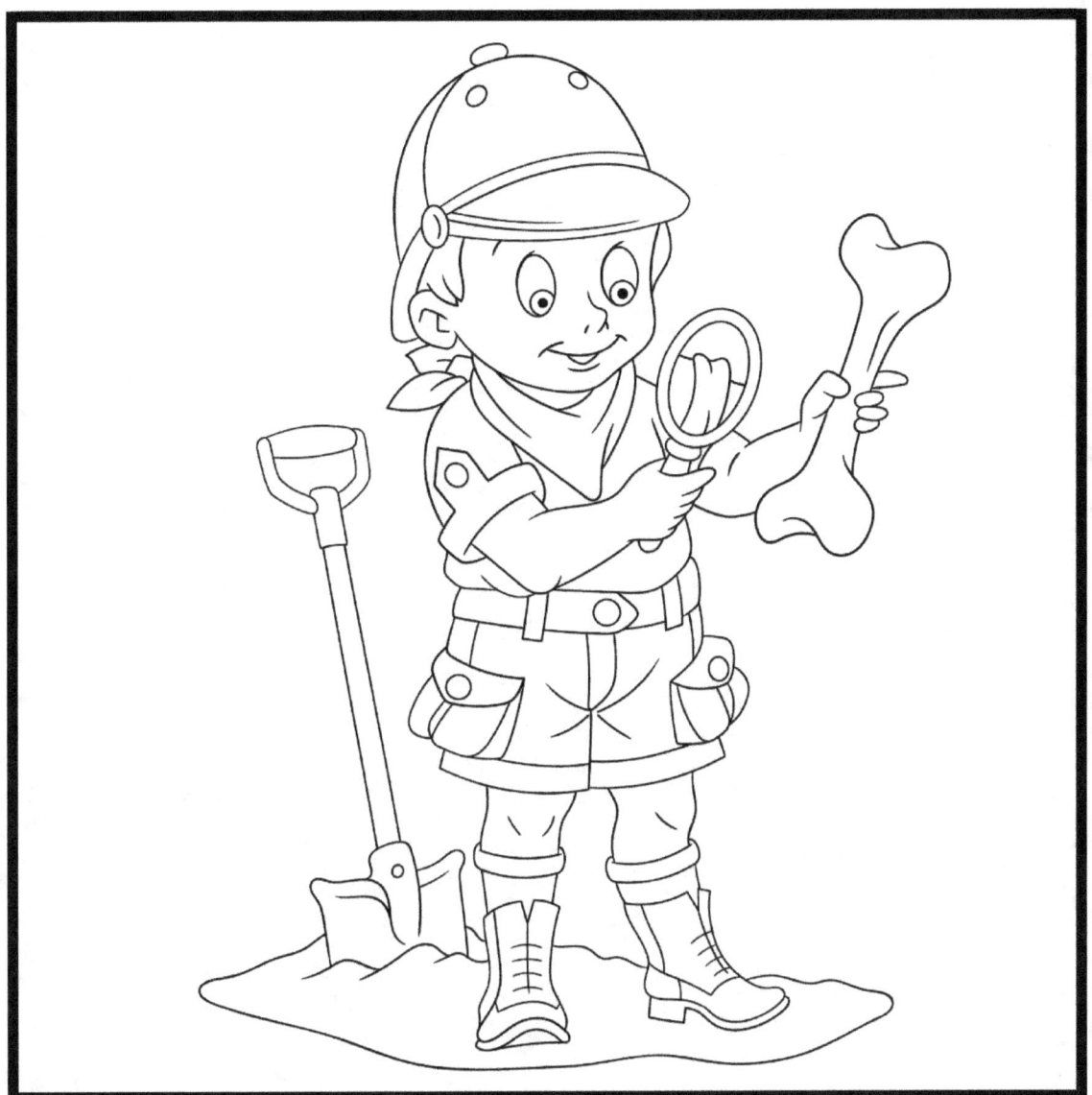

note:

_____

_____

_____

MAY 28TH

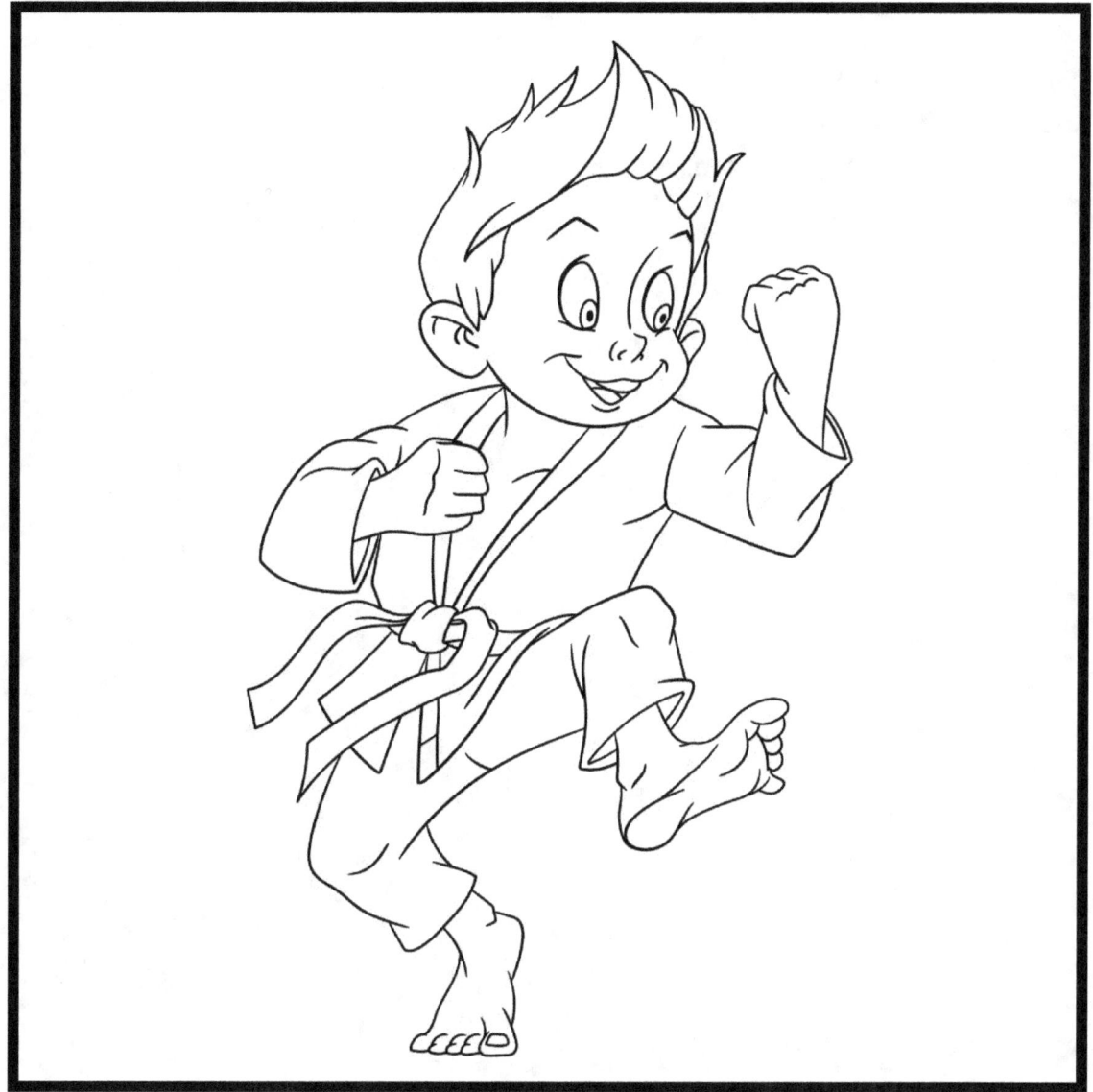

note:

_____

_____

_____

MAY 29TH

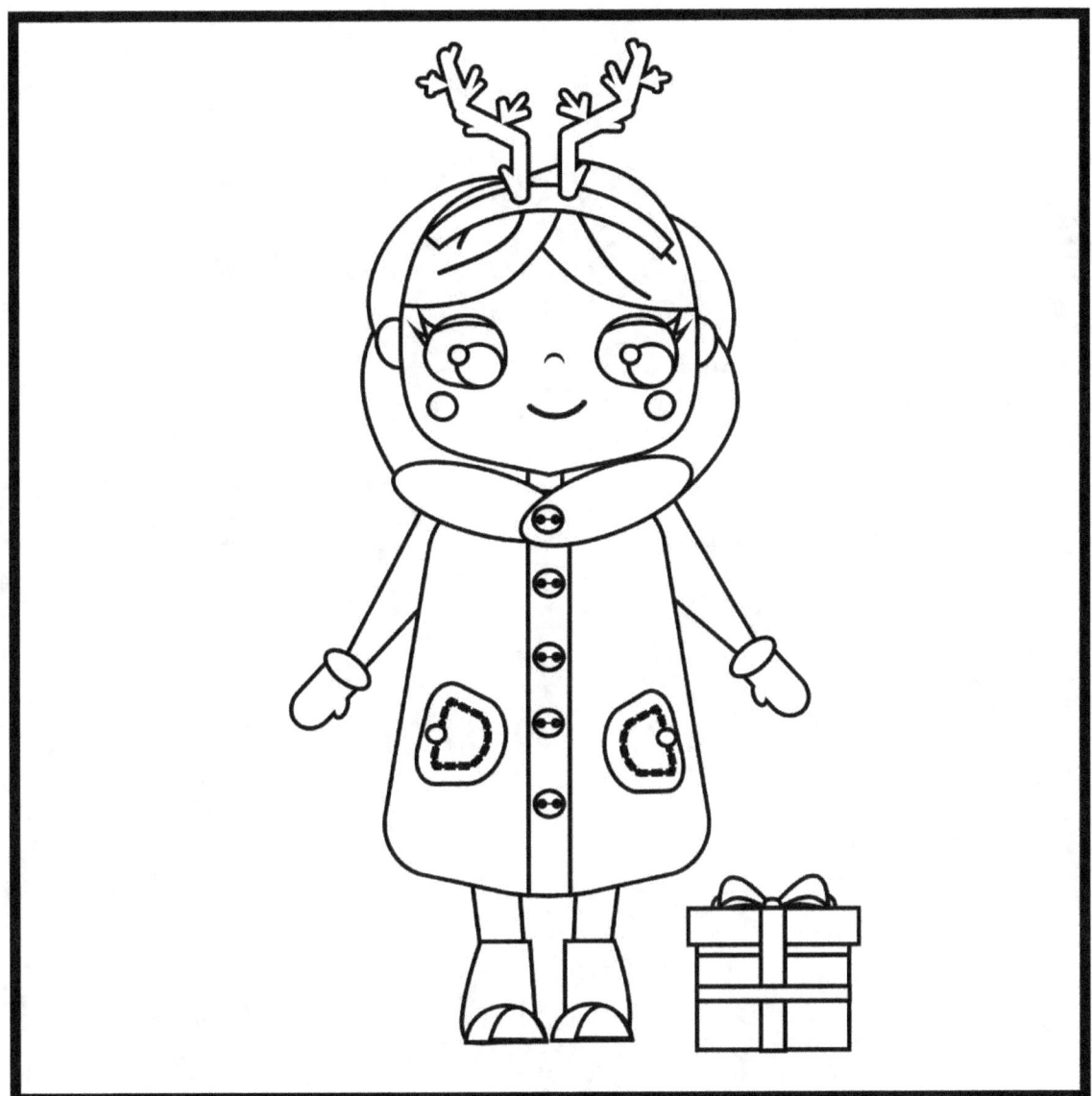

note:

_____

_____

_____

MAY 30TH

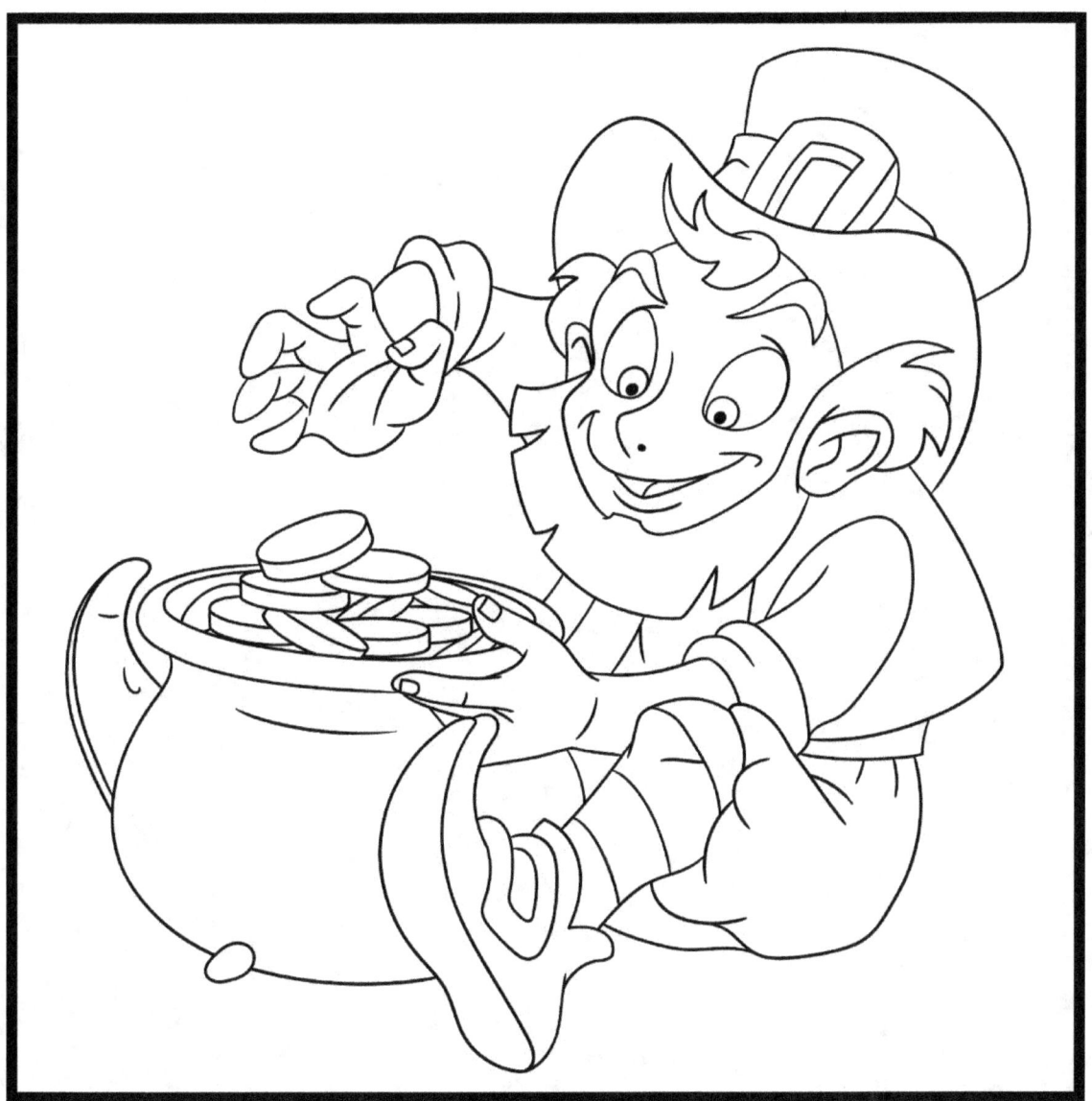

note:

_____

_____

_____

MAY 31TH

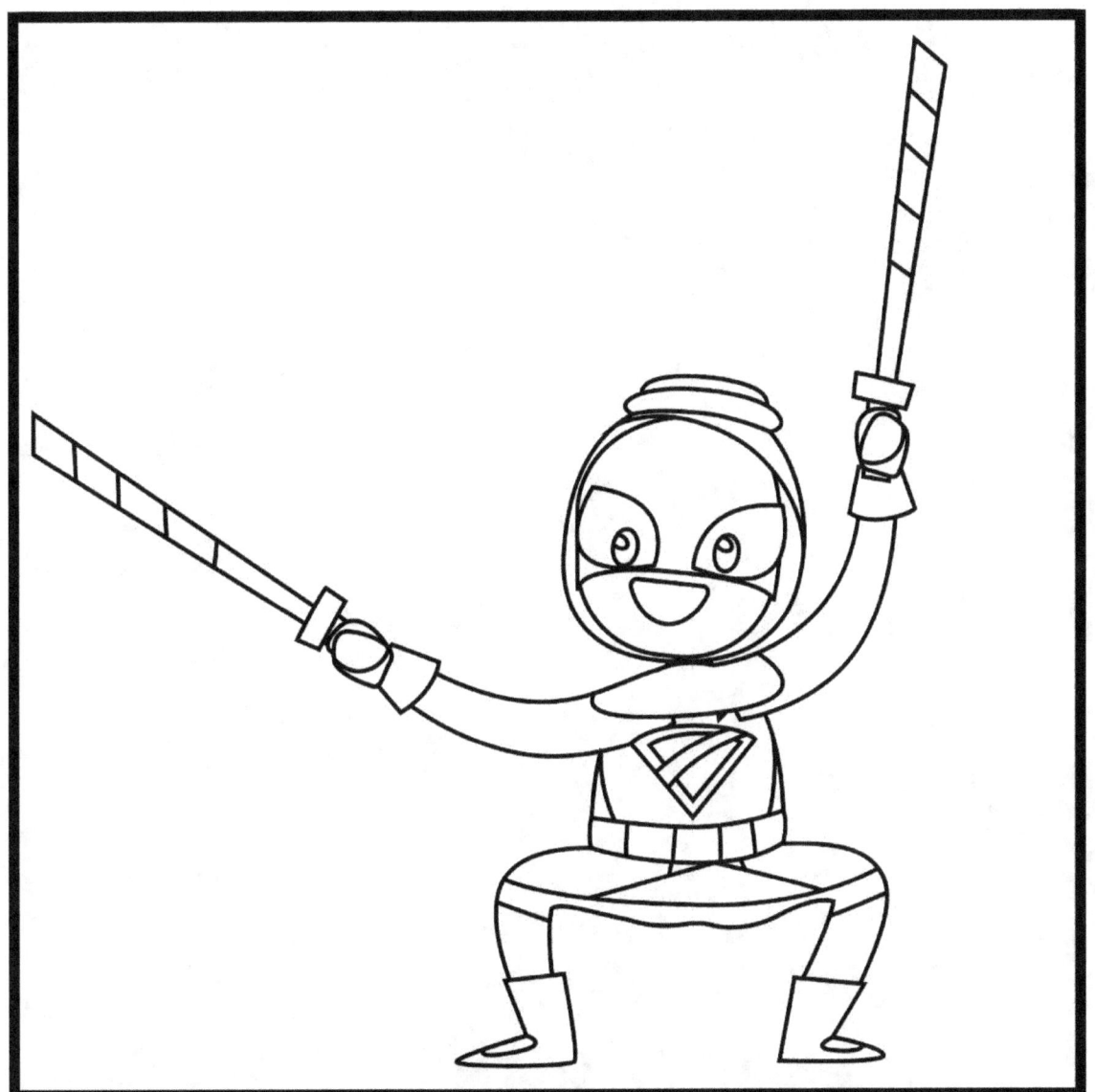

note:

_____

_____

_____

MAY 32TH

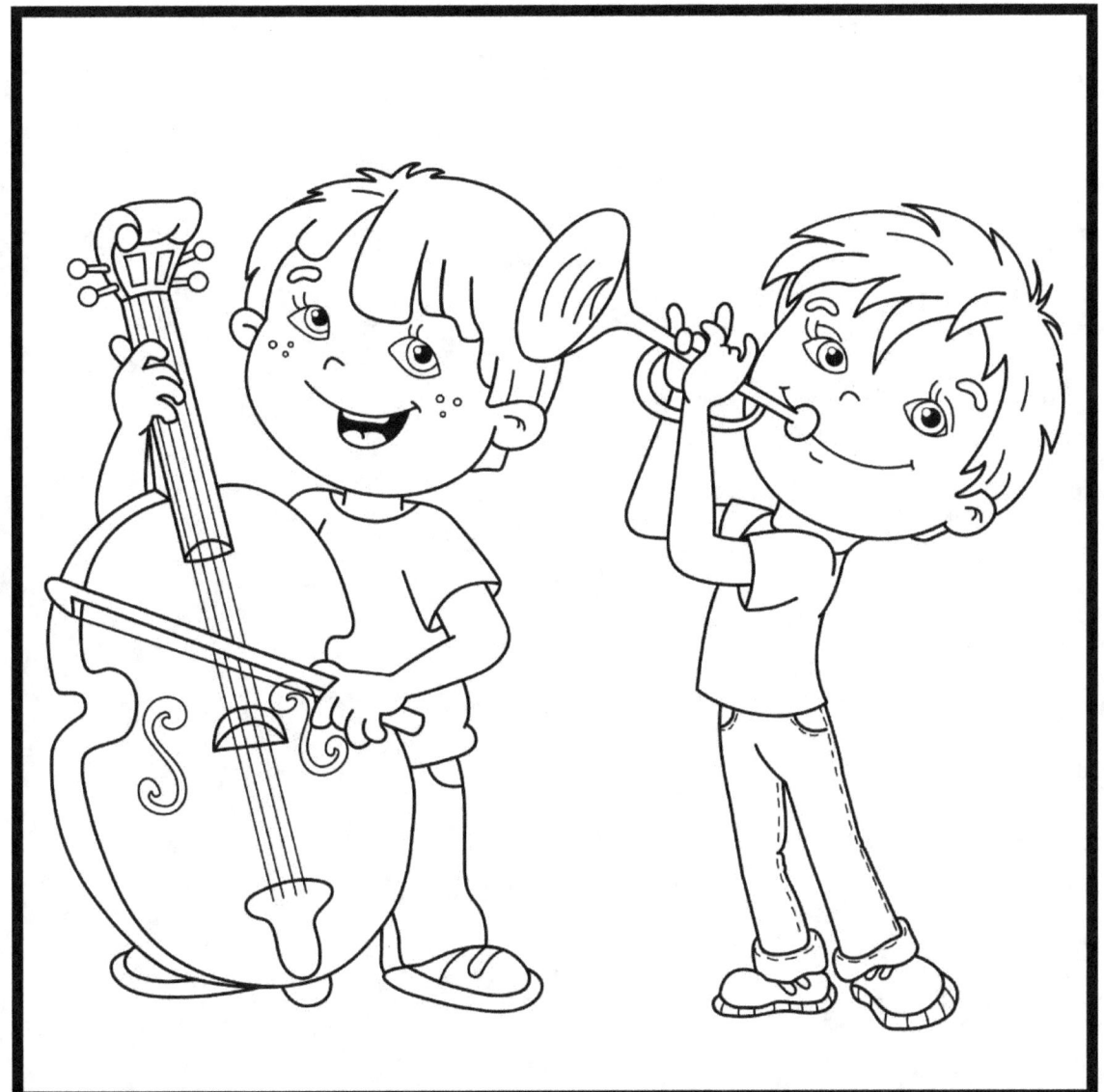

note:

_____

_____

_____

MAY 33TH

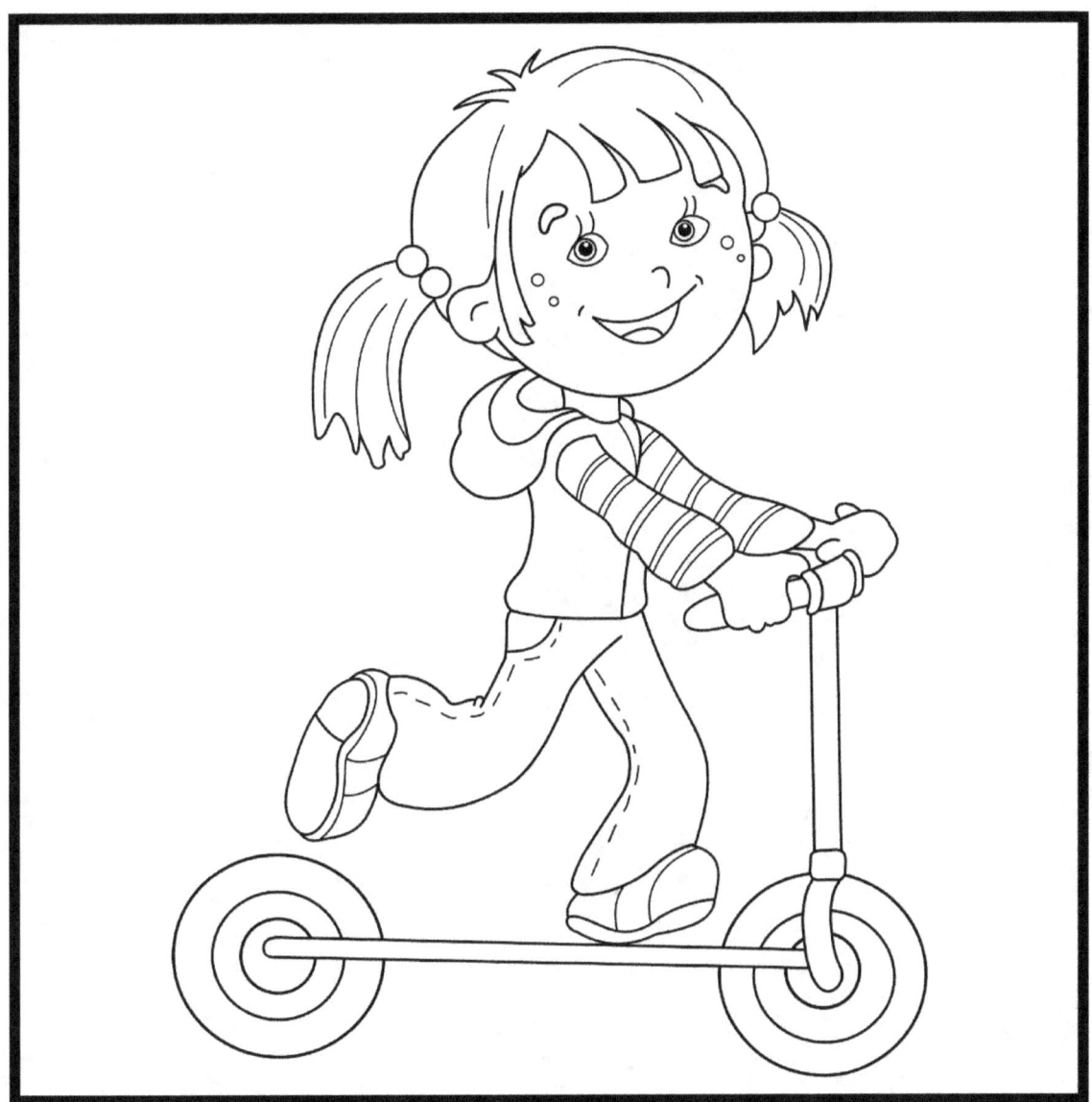

note:

_____

_____

_____

MAY 34TH

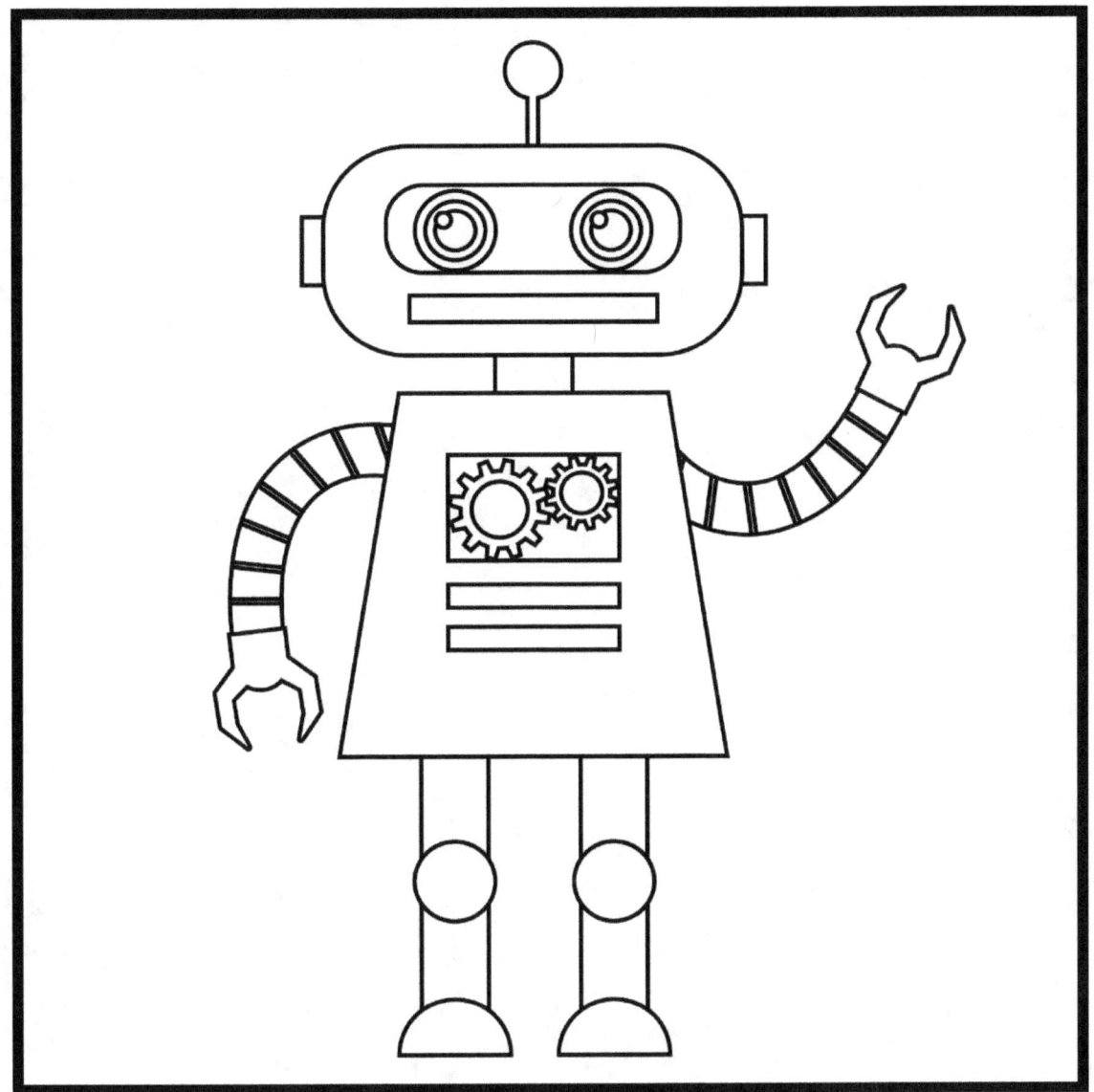

note:

_____

_____

_____

MAY 35TH

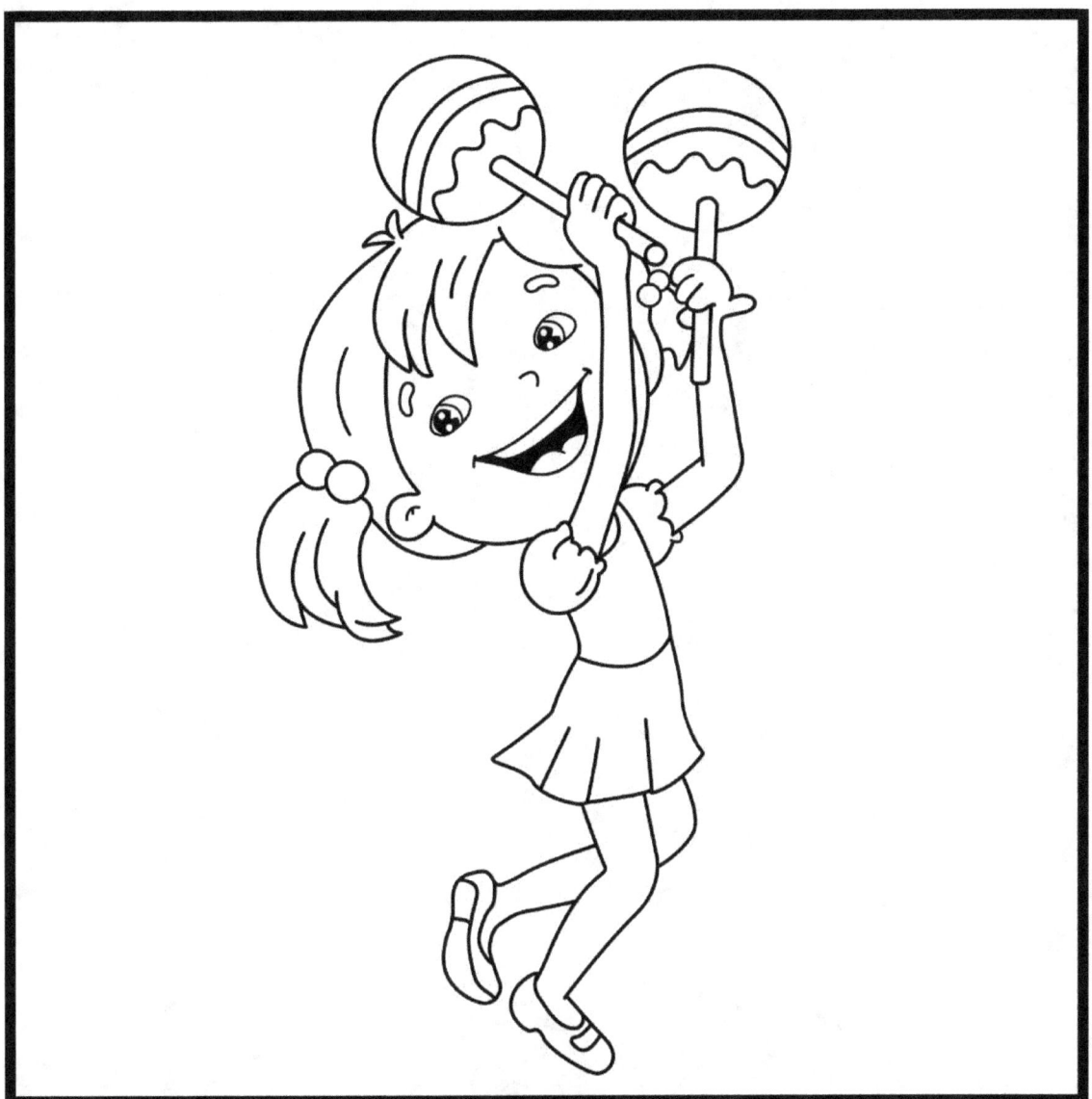

note:

_____

_____

_____

MAY 36TH

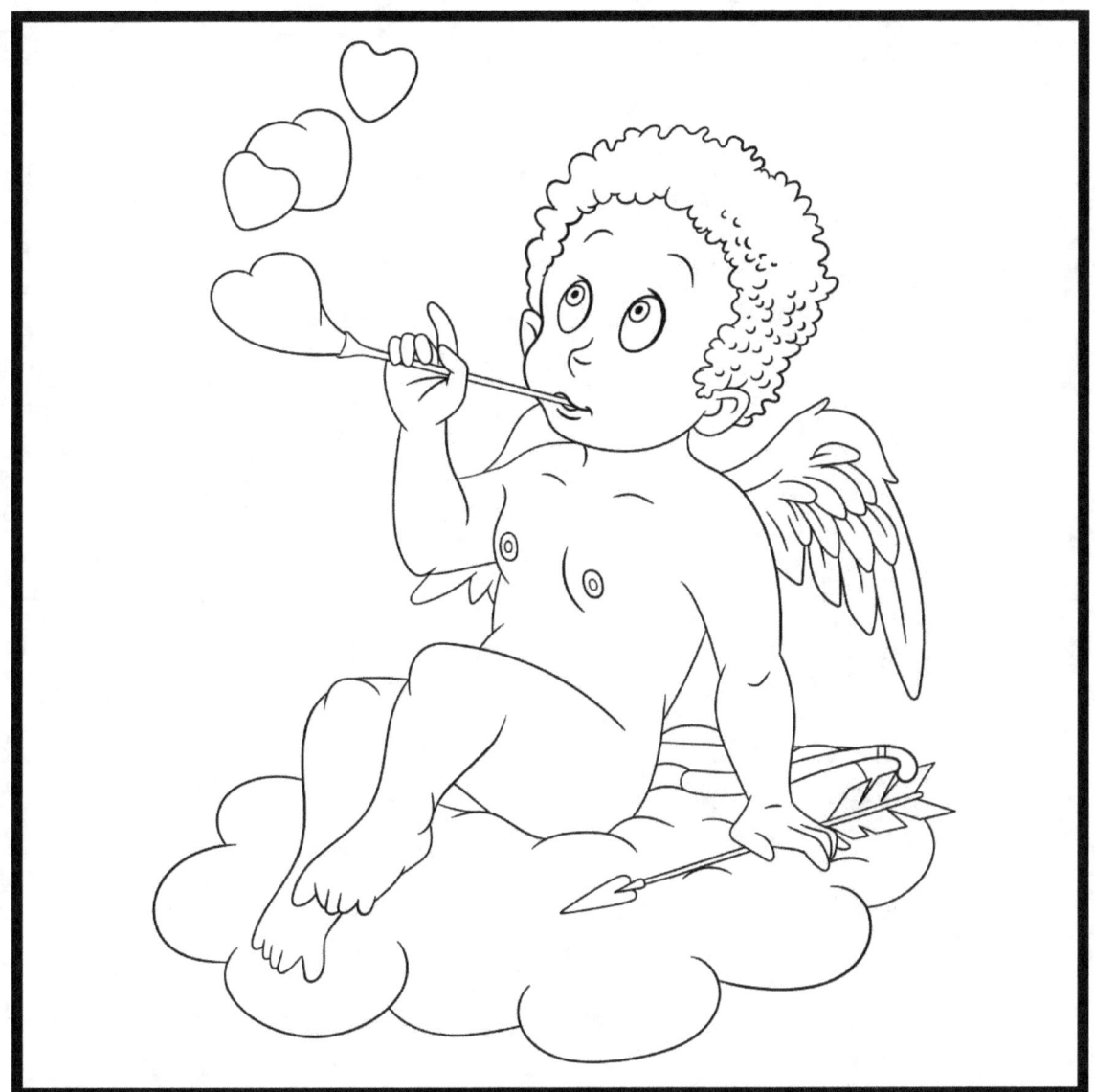

note:

_____

_____

_____

MAY 37TH

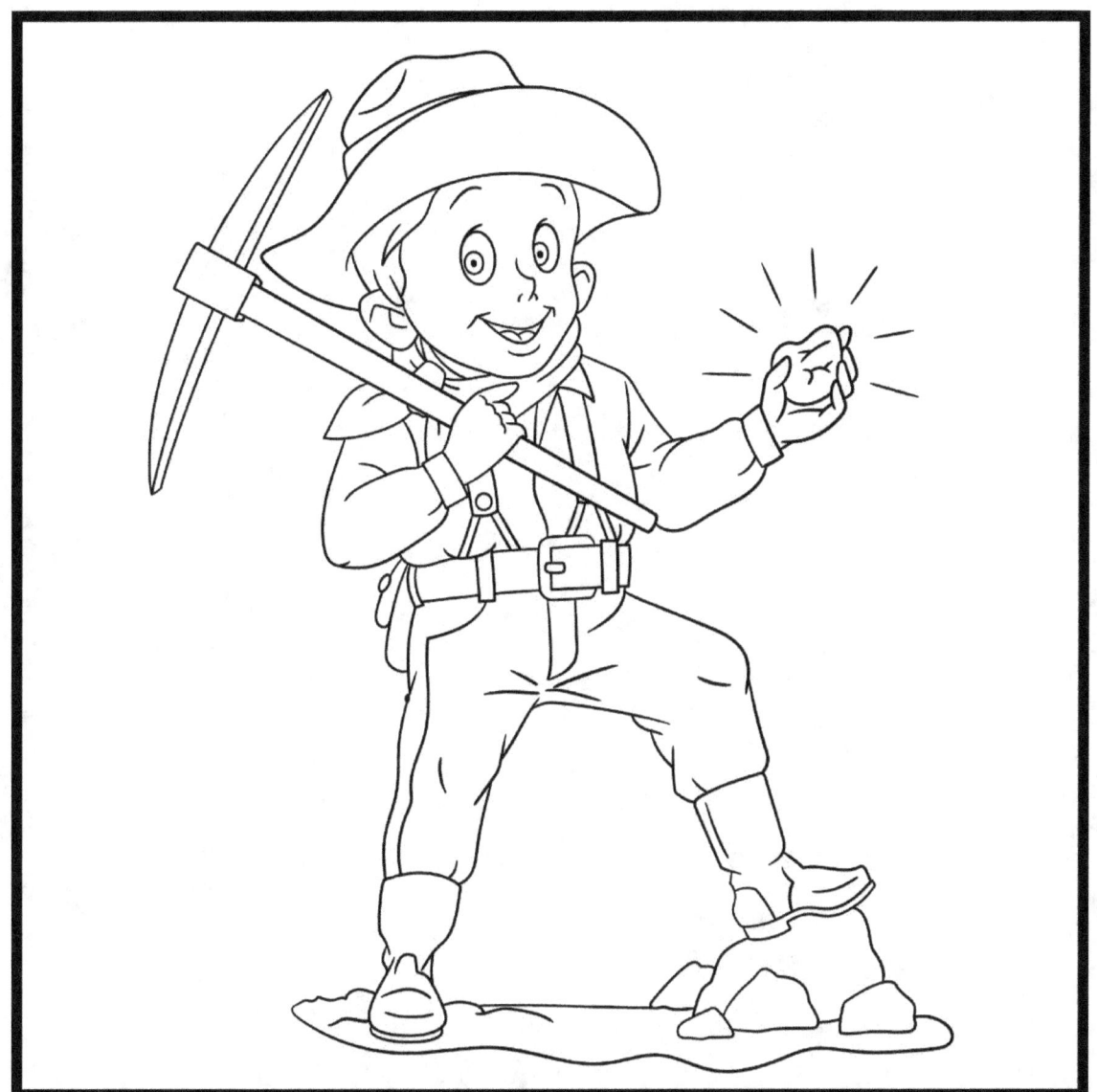

note:

_____

_____

_____

MAY 38TH

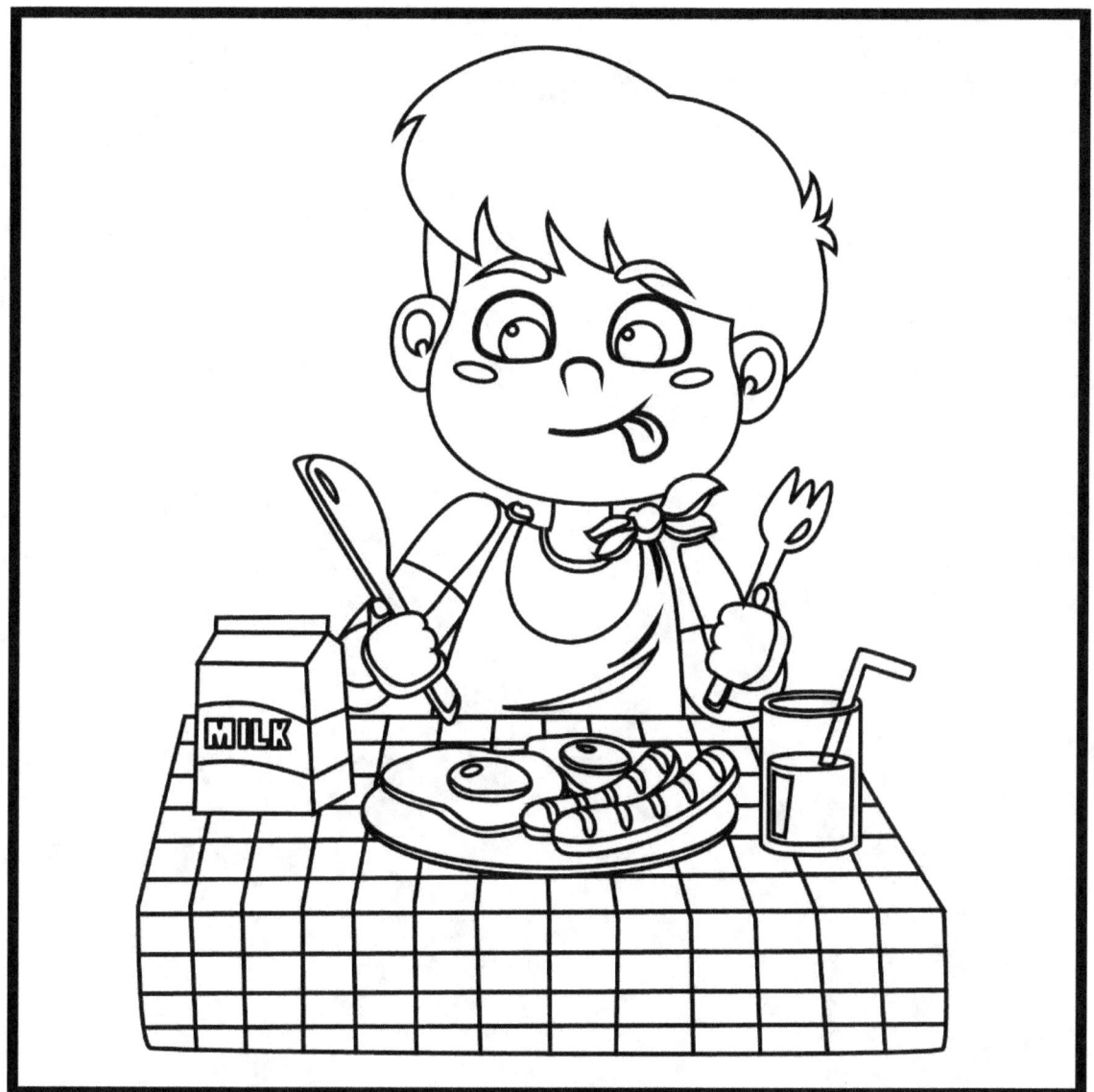

note:

_____

_____

_____

MAY 39TH

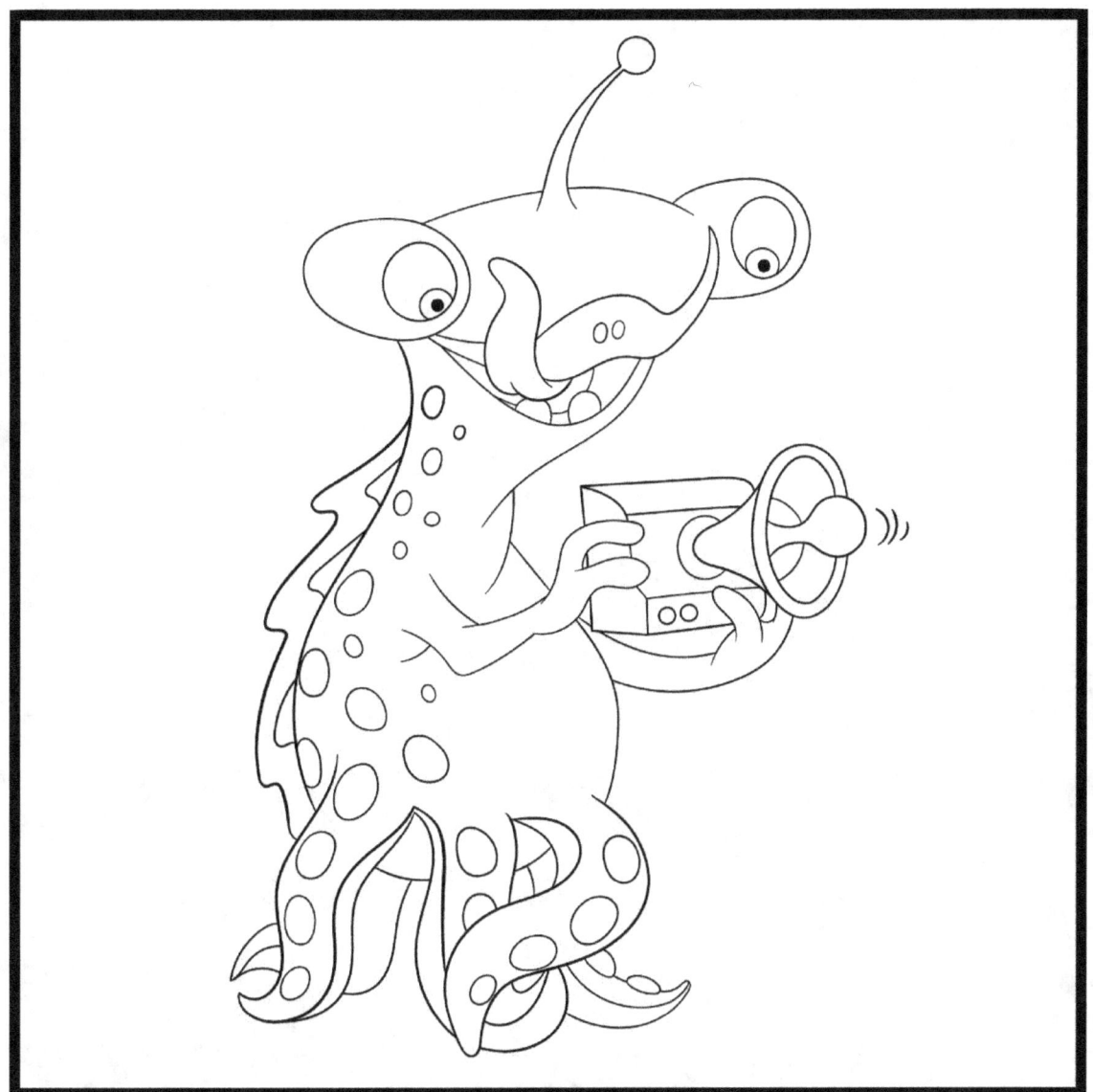

note:

_____

_____

_____

MAY 40TH

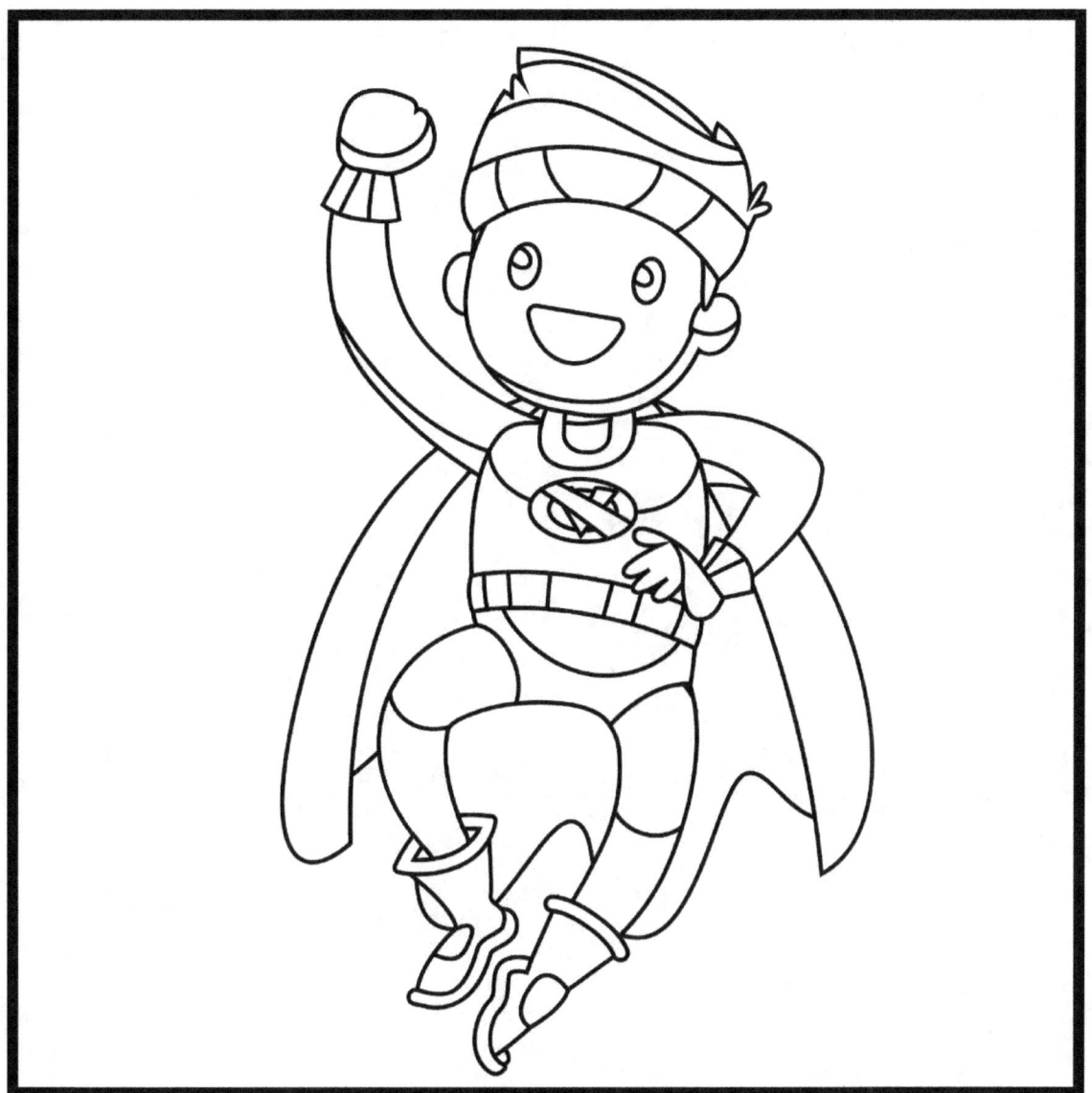

note:

_____

_____

_____

MAY 41TH

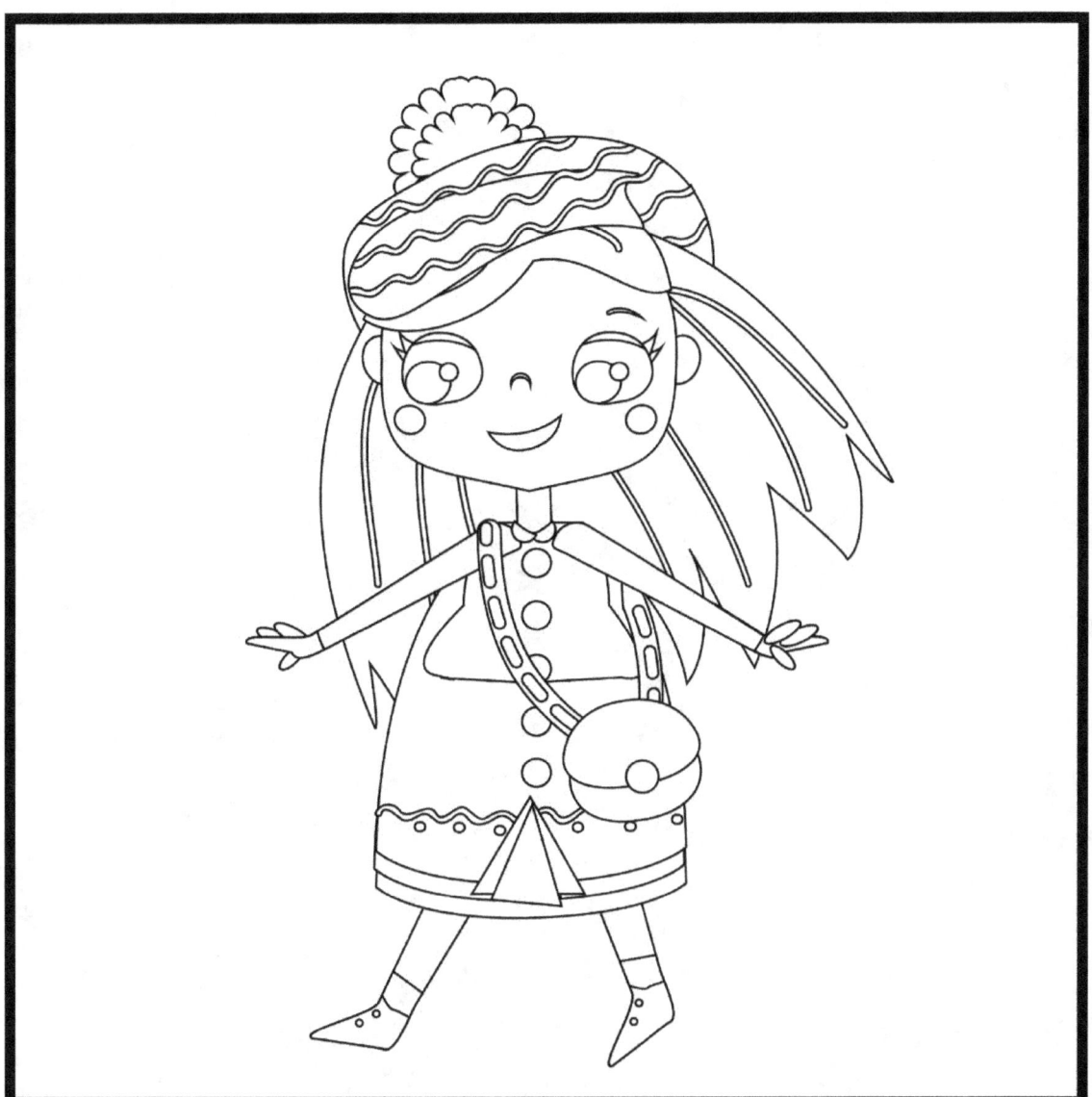

note:

_____

_____

_____

MAY 42TH

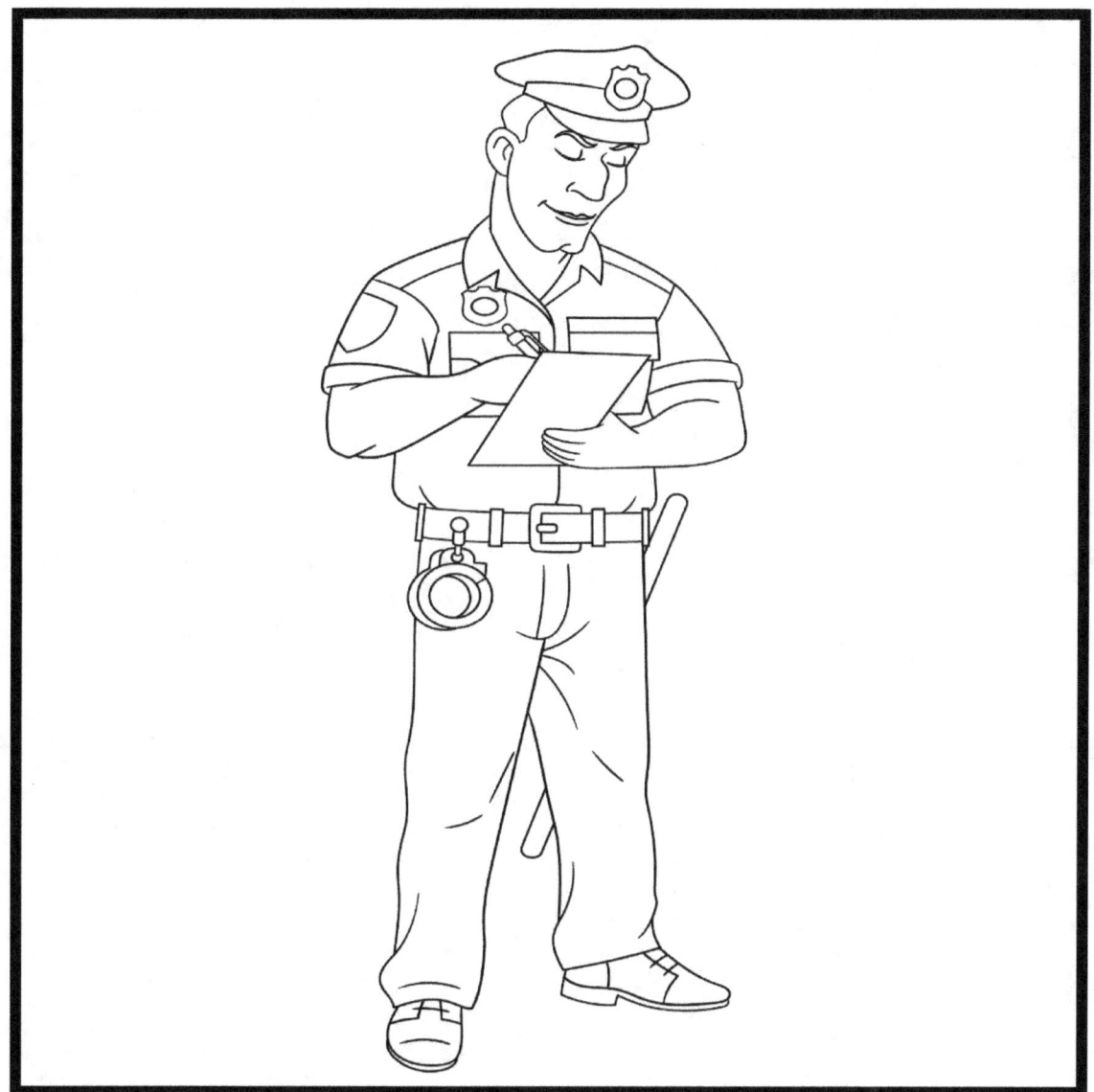

note:

_____

_____

_____

MAY 43TH

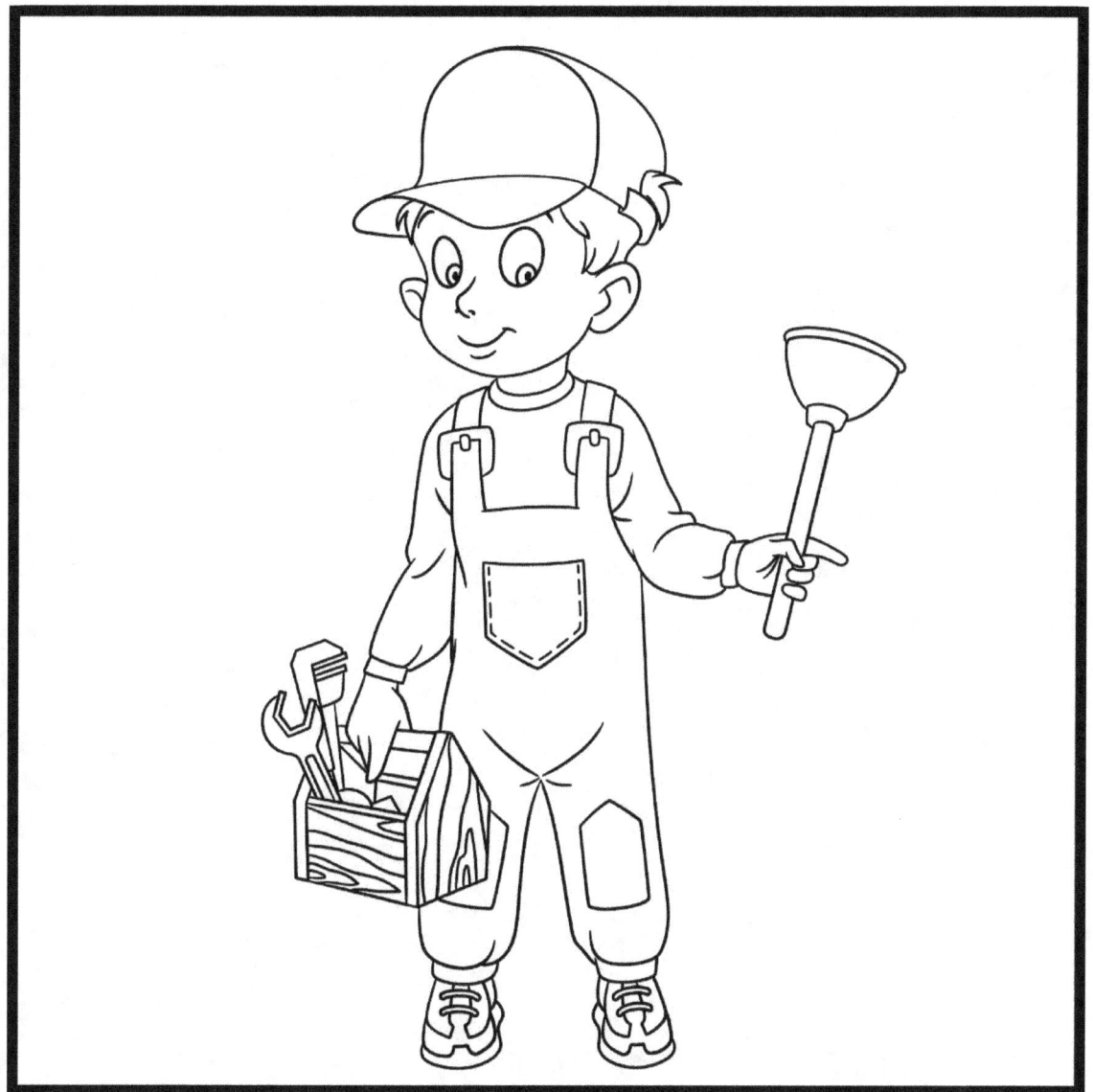

note:

_____

_____

_____

MAY 44TH

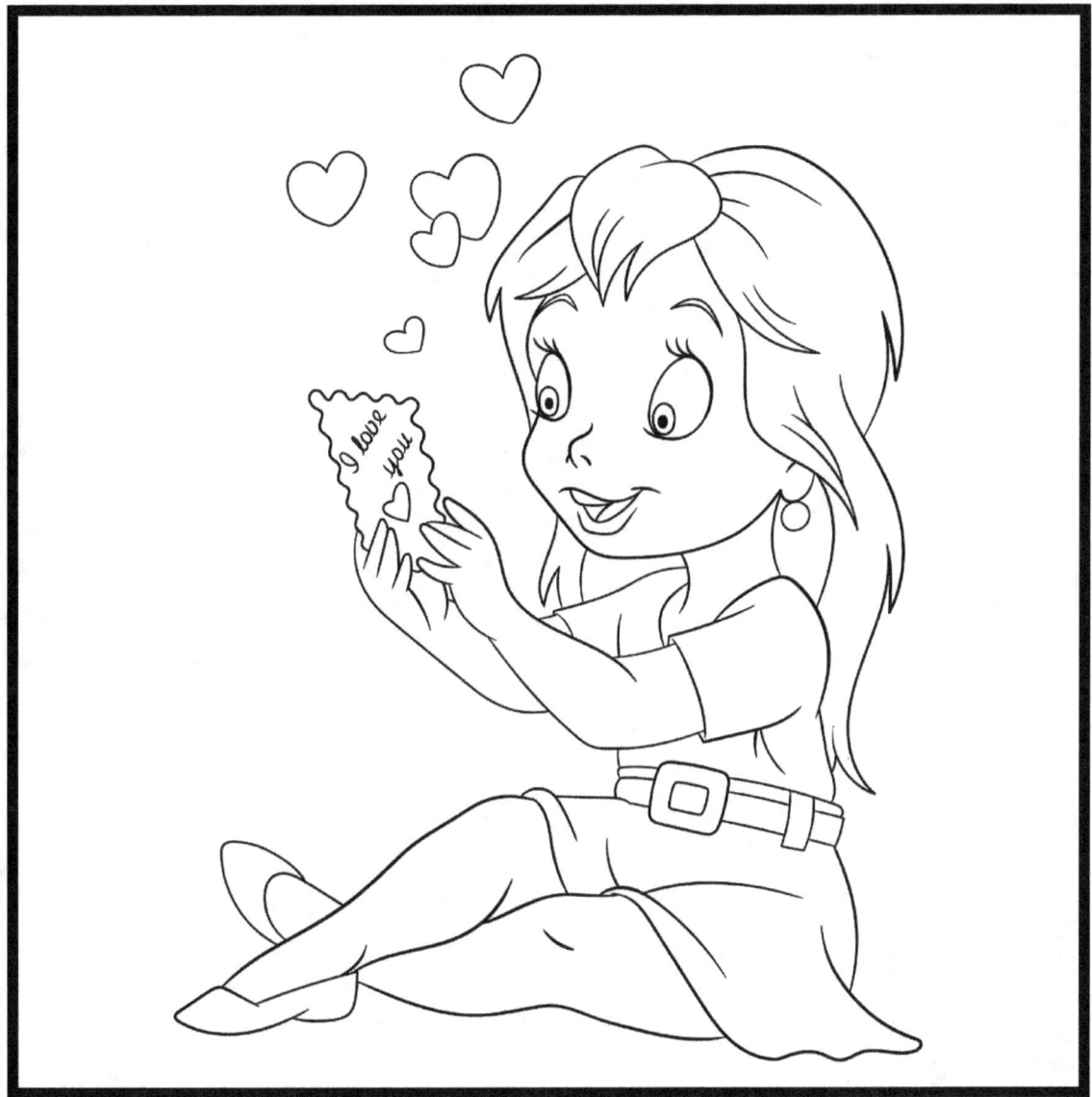

note:

_____

_____

_____

MAY 45TH

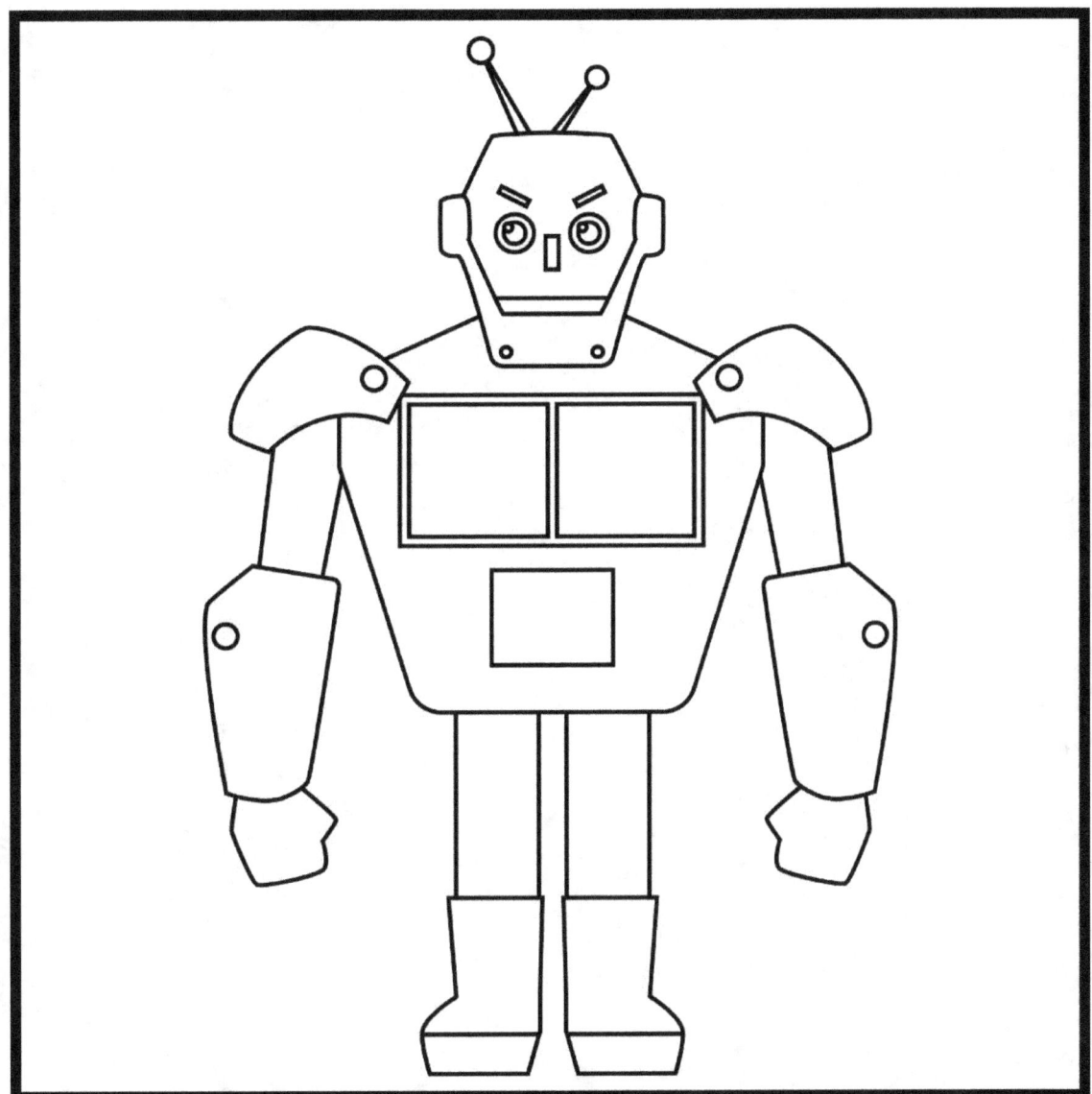

note:

_____

_____

_____

MAY 46TH

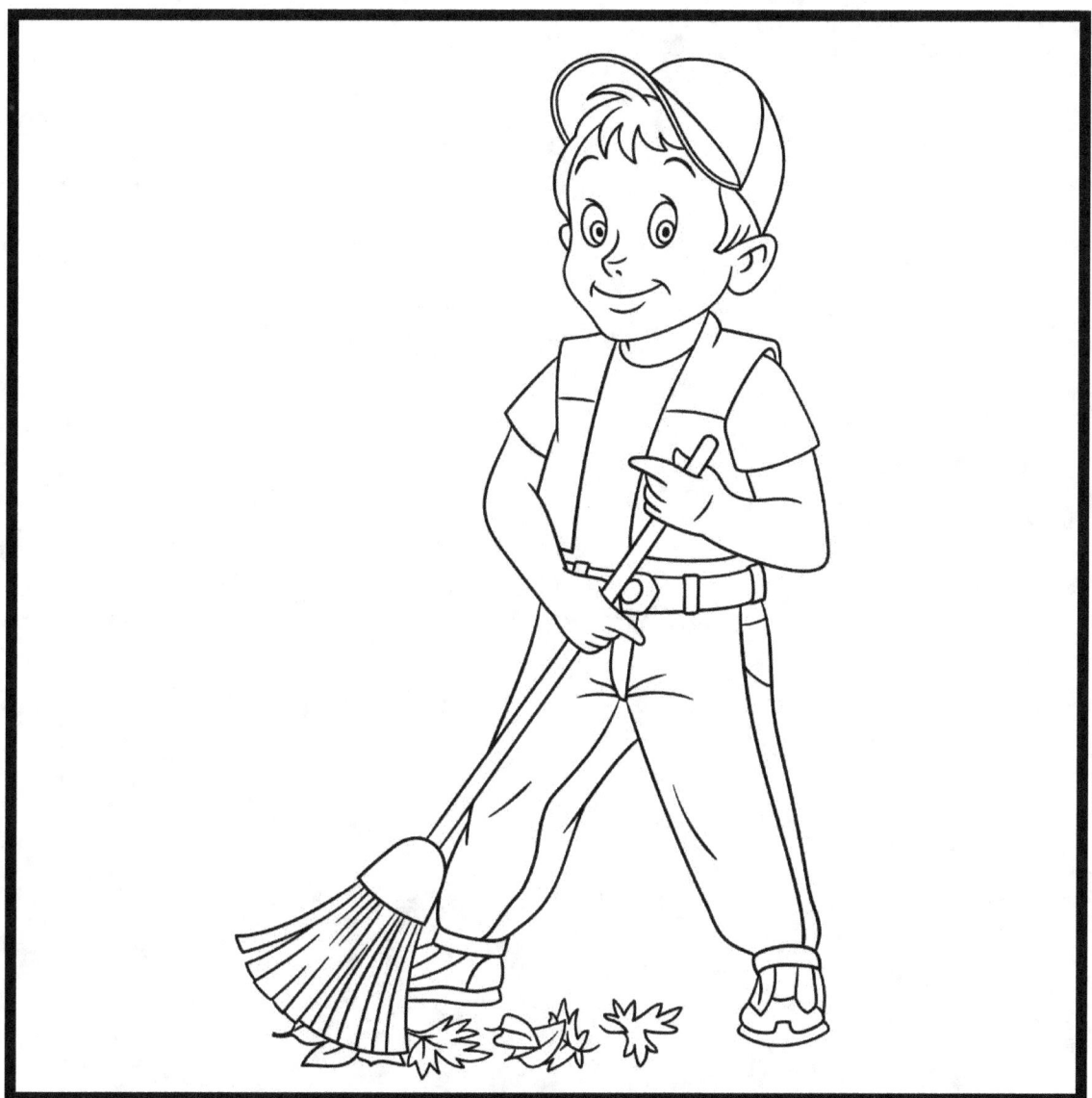

note:

_____

_____

_____

MAY 47TH

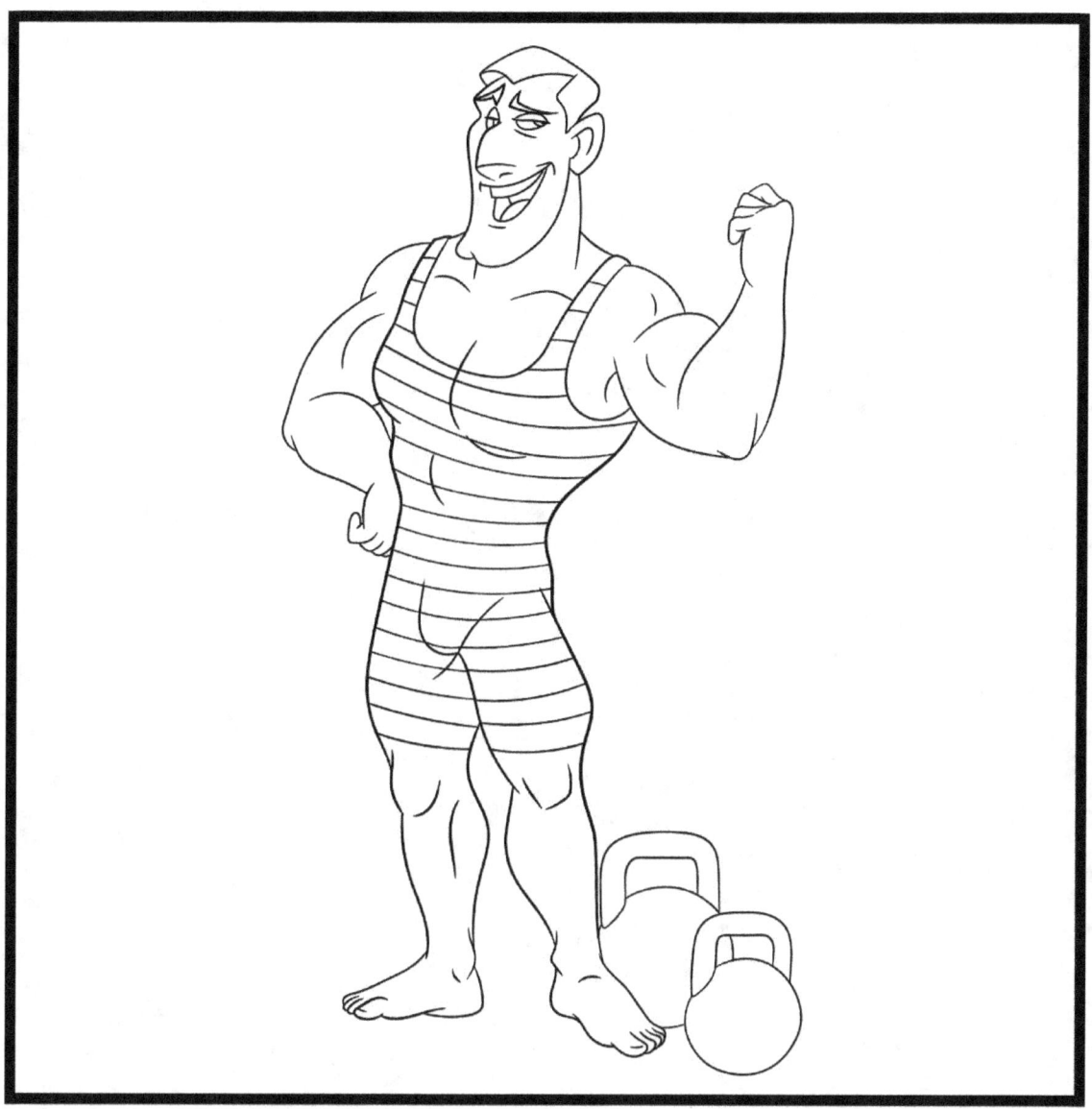

note:

_____

_____

_____

MAY 48TH

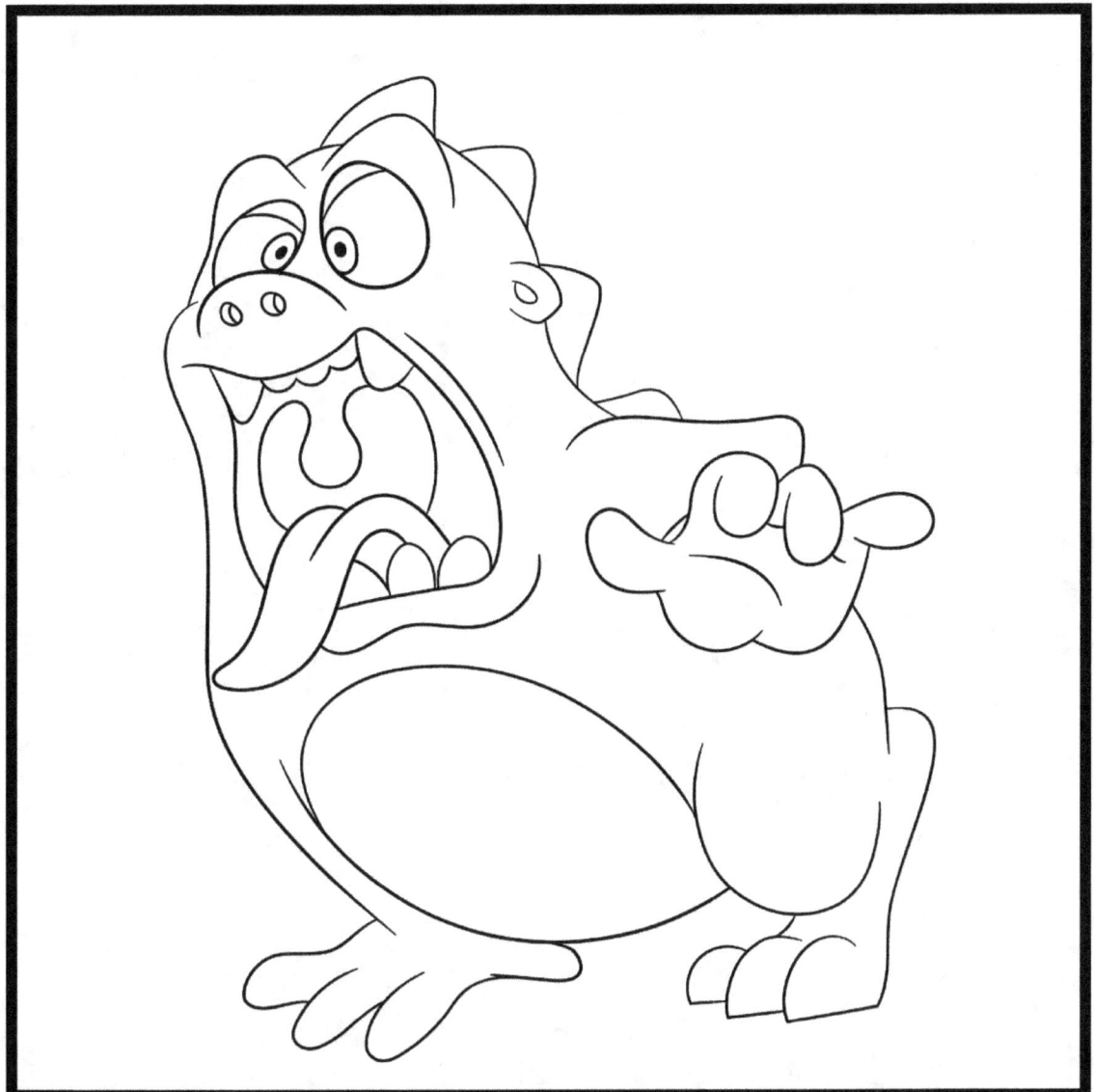

note:

_____

_____

_____

MAY 49TH

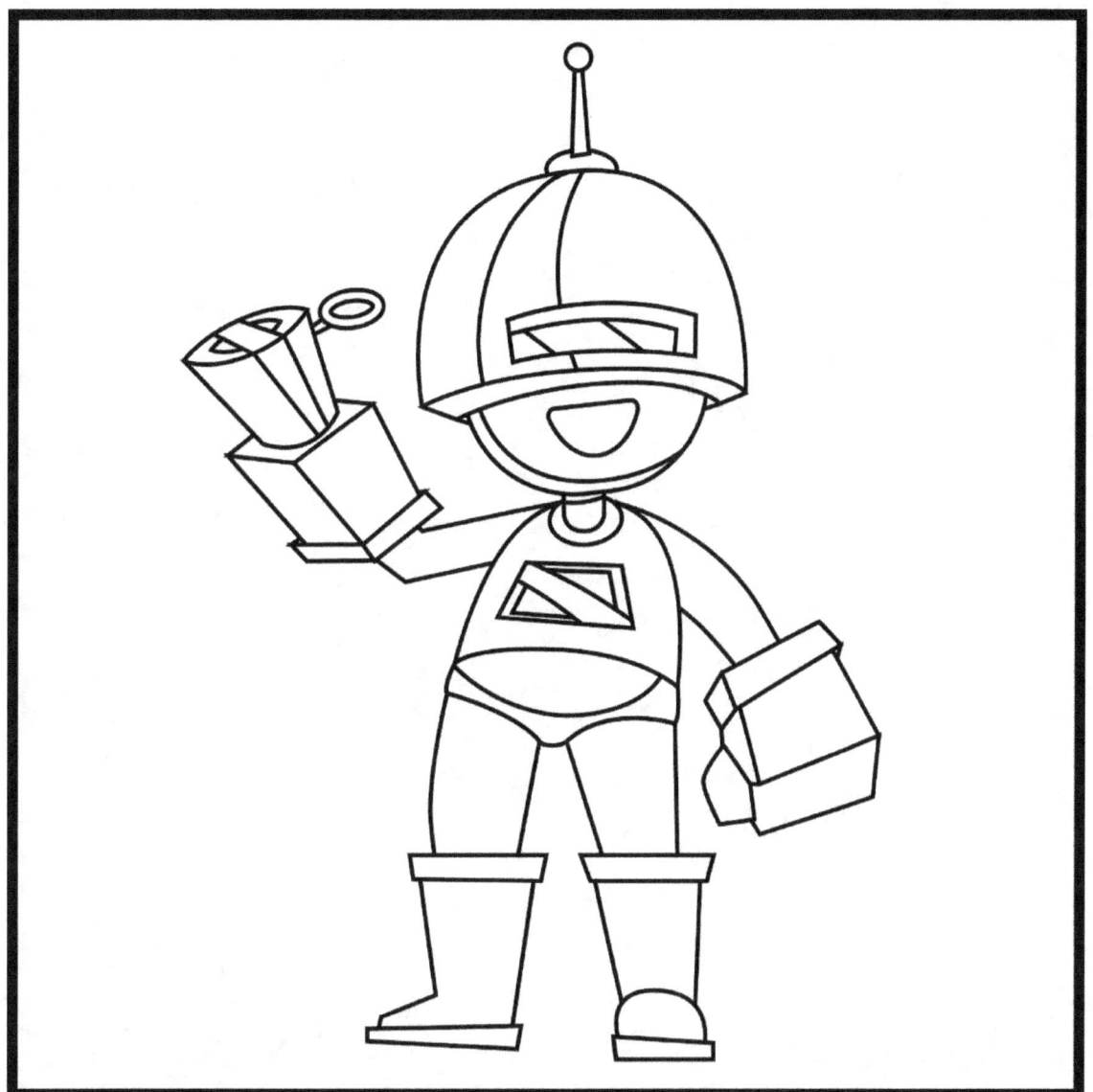

note:

_____

_____

_____

MAY 50TH

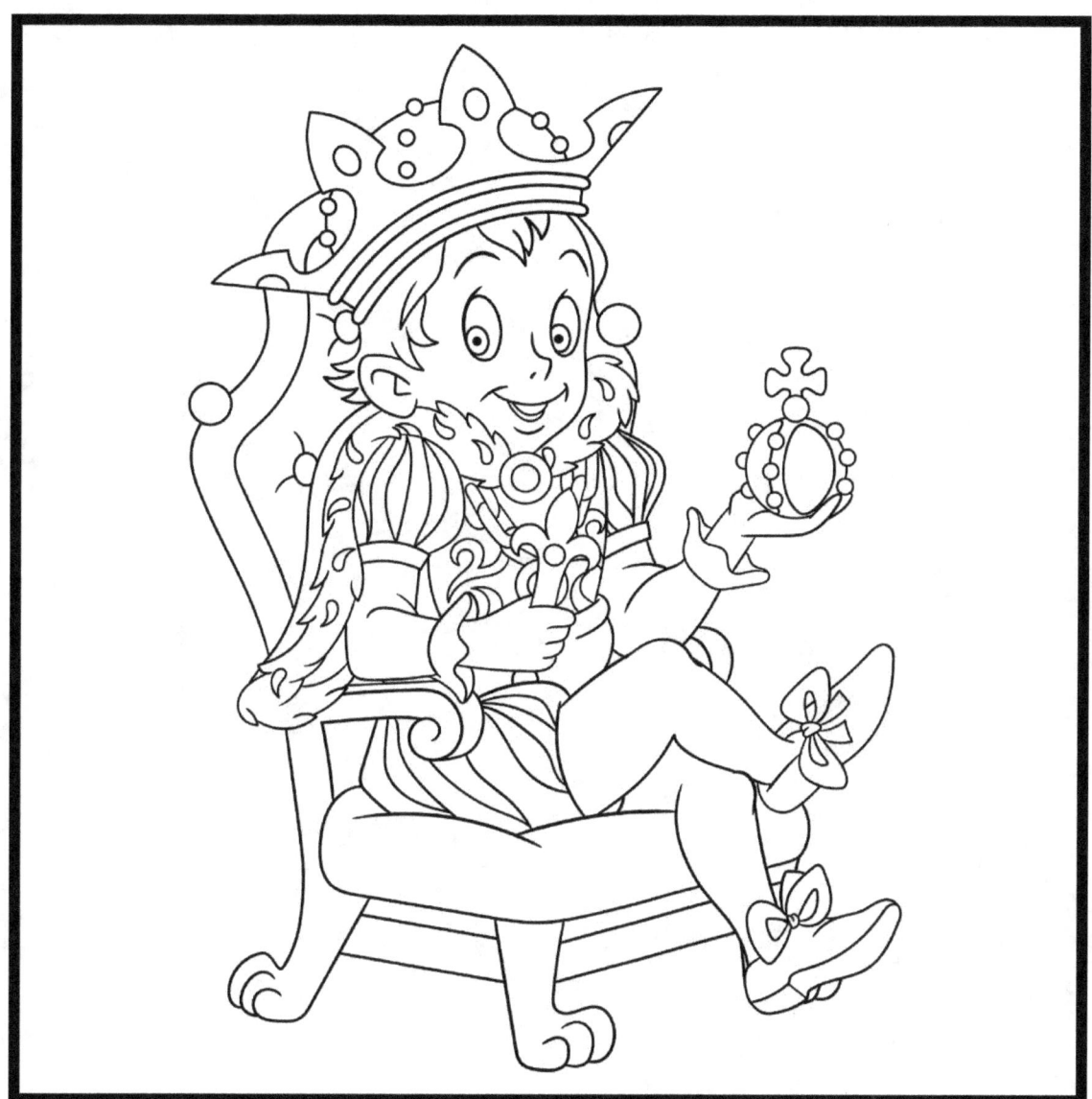

note:

_____

_____

_____

www.ingramcontent.com/pod-product-compliance
Lightning Source LLC
Chambersburg PA
CBHW081606220526

45468CB00010B/2789

*9 7 8 1 9 8 4 1 0 2 4 2 3 *